Refiguring History

What is the status of history in our postmodern world? Why should we study the past if it ultimately remains elusive?

In this engagingly written sequel to *Rethinking History*, Keith Jenkins argues for a refiguration of historical study. At the core of his survey lies the realisation that objective and disinterested histories as well as historical 'truth' are unachievable. The past and questions about the nature of history therefore remain interminably open to new and disobedient approaches.

Jenkins reassesses conventional history in a bold fashion. This committed and radical study presents new ways of 'thinking history', a new methodology and philosophy and their impact on historical practice. The volume is written for students and teachers of history, illuminating and changing the core of their 'discipline'.

Keith Jenkins is Professor of Historical Theory at University College, Chichester. He is the author of *Rethinking History* (1991), *On 'What Is History?'* (1995), *The Postmodern History Reader* (1997), and *Why History?* (1999).

Refiguring History

New thoughts on an old discipline

Keith Jenkins

Routledge
Taylor & Francis Group

LONDON AND NEW YORK

First published 2003
by Routledge
11 New Fetter Lane, London EC4P 4EE

Simultaneously published in the USA and Canada
by Routledge
29 West 35th Street, New York, NY 10001

Routledge is an imprint of the Taylor & Francis Group

© 2003 Keith Jenkins

Typeset in Garamond by MHL Typesetting Limited, Coventry
Printed and bound in Great Britain by TJ International Limited, Padstow

British Library Cataloguing in Publication Data
A catalogue record for this book is available from the British Library

Library of Congress Cataloging in Publication Data
Jenkins, Keith, 1943–
  Refiguring history: new thoughts on an old discipline / Keith Jenkins.
    p. cm.
  Includes bibliographical references and index.
  1. History—Philosophy. 2. Historiography. 3. Historicism. I. Title.

D16.8 J385 2003
901—dc21   2002068251

ISBN 0-415-24410-2 (hbk)
ISBN 0-415-24411-0 (pbk)

For Sue Morgan – with much love

Perhaps, if the future existed, concretely and individually, as something that could be discerned by a better brain, the past would not be so seductive: its demands would be balanced by those of the future. Persons might then straddle the middle stretch of the see-saw when considering this or that object. It might be fun.

(V. Nabokov, *Transparent Things)*

Contents

Acknowledgements

I would like to thank Alun Munslow for supporting the 'idea' of this text and for his encouraging reading of the final draft of it. Beverley Southgate also read the penultimate and final drafts and his meticulous attention to detail and generous comments are appreciated enormously; it is nice to have friends like these. Victoria Peters at Routledge supported the book throughout and her continuing enthusiasm for projects such as this goes well beyond what could normally be expected of an editor. Carole Farnfield once again managed to decipher my handwriting and to patiently produce a typescript that I never quite got right the first time around. Above all, however, I would like to thank Sue Morgan who came into my life quite unexpectedly and, with her love and beautiful friendship, totally transformed it. As a historian herself, her ability to express ideas with a lucidity I can only envy, made me think of things in ways that would never have dawned on me had I written alone. This book is for her; I hope she likes it.

Introduction

> Critical theory of history tries to change the rules of writing history
> or even to ask if any game of writing about history is *worth it*. That is
> a harsh thing to say, but the ... theorists discussed below were in
> agreement that after 2,500 years of *misrepresentation* by historians,
> by the sheer hit and miss of historical representation, by the
> transformation of *after the factness* into a *resource* for control of
> the future, that it was time to consider not playing that game. Not
> historical, that's the path of barbarism, isn't it?
>
> (Sande Cohen, *French Theory in America*)

Since 1991 Routledge have published four books in which I have tried to
address the question of 'the nature of history today': *Rethinking History*
(1991), *On 'What is History'? From Carr and Elton to Rorty and White*
(1995), *The Postmodern History Reader* (1997) and *Why History? Ethics
and Postmodernity* (1999). In the first three of these works I promoted
what I called a postmodern approach towards historicising the past on
the basis that it was the best available in our current cultural condition,[1]
whilst in the fourth I took the discussion somewhat further. In *Why
History?* I argued that whilst it may well be the case that postmodern
approaches still offer the best way to both read and write histories, in
the rich acts of the imagination provided by theorists who are *not*
historians (for example Roland Barthes, Michel Foucault, Jean
Baudrillard, Jean-François Lyotard, Judith Butler, Alain Badiou,
Elizabeth Ermarth *et al.*)[2] and who in that sense do not much need
history, we now have enough intellectual power to begin to work for

an individual and social emancipatory future *without* it. In terms of
critical and empowering thinking, my argument went, historians may
no longer have much to say to a culture that now seems too late still to
be modern and which is arguably so ahistorical in its practices such that
modernist ways of doing history, whether in its ideological (upper-case
metanarrative) or academic (lower-case professional) modes, may well
be coming to a close. In a really very tangible sense postmodernism thus
seemed to me to signal the end of at least these sorts of conceptualisa-
tions of history and, maybe, even the end of thinking historically at all.
And I argued that, in the light of the alternative discourses offered by
the range of cultural and philosophical thinkers I have mentioned, this
could be considered 'a good thing'.

It is from what one might call this 'end of history' position – and
various resistances to it – that the arguments of this book primarily
emerge. For on the whole I remain unconvinced by counter-arguments
which continue to stress the crucial importance of a historical consciousness as a personal and social necessity (for example, those by
Arthur Marwick in his *The New Nature of History*) or by those panic-
mongers who insist that, shorn of epistemological, methodological and
ethical foundations, history will slide helplessly down the slippery slope
of postmodern relativism and scepticism towards the much-threatened
and apparent 'disaster of nihilism' (thus Richard Evans in his *In Defence
of History*).[3] And yet, at the same time, I am aware that despite my own
position with regard to the possibly *passé* nature of history, the study of
'proper', professional, academic history – the sole object of my
attention in this text – still continues in higher education and still
displays the appearance of occasional vitality. And I am also conscious
that for many history tutors and students the message has still not been
received that, if history is to continue for a while despite its somewhat
moribund state, then what life it may have still *ought* to be articulated
through the reflexive foregrounding of a postmodern discourse wedded
to the idea of emancipation. And so in this text I try to put before those
students of history who are about to become or who are already engaged
in 'doing history' three sets of what I hope are new arguments for
considering it in the way I suggest. These are arguments which stand in
critical disobedience to the norms of mainstream professional historical
theory and practice and which try to breathe what fresh air can be

breathed into an 'old discipline' by refiguring it into a discourse that gratefully accepts and celebrates what will be referred to throughout as the inevitable failures of historical representation/presentation rather than striving to overcome them. These three sets of arguments I develop in three chapters. First, in Chapter 1, 'Opening time(s)', I put forward a series of general, theoretical reflections drawn from the French theorist Jacques Derrida and others considerably influenced by him. Together, these are thinkers who are presented here as favouring endless openness and thus endless historical (historians') interpretive differences, problematisations, uncertainties and dilemmas for sound political reasons. And there is a subtle but significant point to be made here, for despite the fact that most historians now embrace a version of interpretive pluralism in their work, I will argue that this is not the same agenda as that favoured by postmodern perspectives. For no matter how many 'differing interpretations' they may admit to, most mainstream historians still continue to strive for 'real historical knowledge', for objectivity, for the evidentially-based synoptic account and for truth-at-the-end-of-enquiry; in other words, for what are effectively interpretive *closures*. And I will propose the exact opposite: that in the name of interminable openness and unthought possibilities we *ought* to have an implacable opposition to every type of closure on at least two counts. First, because at the level of the historical text it just happens to be the case that interminable openness is logically unavoidable: there is no way that any historical closure can ever be achieved – that is certain. And second, because such unavoidable openness allows for new, disrespectful, contentious, radical readings and rereadings, writings and rewritings of the past ('the before now') to be produced – and this is excellent. The reasons for this desirable refiguring *ad infinitum* are spelt out in detail in the following chapters, but the overtly political thinking which informs them can be summarised now in a prefacing kind of way so that it can be kept in mind right from the start.

I hold that for people (subjects) to be inserted into, grow up and live in, any given social and cultural formation, then such socialisation or enculturation never runs smoothly, and, more importantly, is never fully accomplished, so that the sometime identity which subjects inhabit is always temporary and thus always becoming other than it is.

What constitutes (makes up) the human subject at any given moment in space and time is therefore not the expression of some inner core or human 'essence', but rather the result of that dynamic process termed *iterability* (the process of repetition and difference; of the repetition of the never quite the same) which ensures that nobody is ever complete or stable or fixed 'once and for all'. Here dominant forms of enculturating power are exposed in their failure ever to completely 'stitch up' the 'social individual'. And it is this 'failed' and thus always tense and stress-ful condition, this endless play of unstable becoming at the levels of the personal-political, that gives a radical, disobedient and thus counter-hegemonic (counter-dominant) politics a chance. For if subjects are never complete but are always subjects (or better still, subjectivities) in constant formation, then this instability allows for all kinds of actual personal and social antagonisms and ambivalences. In so far as subjects have identities they can identify with, then, such identities – who we *think* we are – are always temporary balances between our successes and our failures to resolve the tensions we embody.

Similarly, and extending this way of thinking into the realm of the social, no social/cultural formation is any more able to fold into harmonious and fixed relationships the patternings of dominance and subordination which so uneasily constitute it than 'its' individual subjects can resolve the inner tensions of their identities, informed as they are precisely by the ways they are immersed in the social. Thus we can begin to conclude these much abbreviated remarks by saying that at the level of the socio-cultural, as at the level of the subject, no hegemonic (dominant) ordering is ever secure: it is always at risk of being trans-formed; re-figured. Moreover, because no given resolution of any socio-cultural formation or indeed any new counter-settlement is of a 'natural' kind (is not based on any knowable natural and/or 'real' order of things) then no 'settlement' can ever be founded or legitimated on the basis of how we *know* things really are, on epistemological grounds. Accordingly, it is this recognition that no subject or political system is ever totally *closed* that gives radical democracy a chance, the political theorist Ernesto Laclau (for it is his ideas I draw on at this point) stipulating a definition of radical democracy as the attempt to preserve the conflictive character of all personal/social processes so as to stave off a total(itarian) social formation whilst at the same time aiming for a polity of 'equality and equivalence' that will still give difference an opportunity.[4] Consequently, the main aim of this text *is to try to work the discourse of history in the direction of that kind of radical, open-ended democracy that grasps the impossibility of enacting a total historical/historicising closure of the past whilst recognising that its refigured ways of figuring things out 'will never have been good enough'* – and that this is the most desirable thing. In this text I work on the assumption and in the hope that we might still have the chance to aspire to human rights communities despite the failure of the modernist experiment of the 'Enlightenment Project'[5] in those bourgeois and proletarian forms which have now become so exhausted and that the past/post-modern condition we inhabit gives us the chance to refigure and so 'begin again' … not least by refiguring history.

Second, in Chapter 2, 'Last order(s)', I try to show – in the light of the more philosophical arguments put forward in Chapter 1 – that at the level of professional, academic history, there are some very history-specific reasons why interpretive free-play cannot ever be remotely closed down by historians even if they want to which, despite their periodic protestations to the contrary, I think most still do. It is my belief, and my argument here, that there are no non-problematic rules or norms of translation or transcription (as articulated through multifarious methods, skills and practices) which allow the past (all that has happened 'before now') to be truth-fully or objectively or fairly or scientifically represented as 'historical knowledge' at the level of the history text and that this condition, rather than being regrettable, is again the very best thing we can hope for. It really is brilliant news that historians can just never get things right. That their representations and presentations of 'the before now' are always failed representations and presentations. It is liberating for the creative imagination that there is no such thing as a correct historical method and that history can never fulfil its aspiration to be an epistemology (can never fulfil its desire to obtain reliable and objective knowledge). For it is this failure which allows radical otherness to come, new imaginations to emerge. We ought not to waste this chance of otherness, of newness, in deference to the dead weight of professional, academic orthodoxy, even when most generously construed.

Third, in Chapter 3, 'Beginning again: on disobedient disposition', I suggest an attitude towards refigurings of the historicised 'before now' in ways little imagined and little practised. I have said already that I am not at all sure if any sort of historicising discourse still has much of a resonance in our social formation; I mean, who exactly does it speak to both privately and publicly; who, in the light of the ways in which our subjectivities are formed, can now be 'subjected' to its authority? But if it *is* still desired that something should live on under the old name of history, then it might best be the 'useful fiction' (for as we shall see all histories are fictive — it is their continued value or lack of it that is at issue today) that I suggest in Chapter 3 on the basis of the reasons I have begun to indicate in some of the above paragraphs.

This is not to say that Chapter 3 offers an answer to the frequently asked question of 'what would a postmodern history look like?' There is no blue-print, no template offered here; that would be too modernist, too prefigurative, for words. Rather I outline what might best be called 'favourable dispositions' towards new ways of imagining; a relaxed attitude towards creative failure. What I am advocating in Chapter 3 (and indeed in all the pages which follow) is an attitude of radical and critical disobedience that, as against most historical analyses, seeks no resolution or agreement about historical problematisations but which celebrates the failure of each and every one of them: what is being advocated throughout is an attitude which disregards convention, disobeys the authoritative voice and which replaces any definitive closure with an interminable openness, any exhaustive ending with an et cetera, and any full stop with an ellipsis...

I now wish to make two final, introductory comments. The first is that although this book comes very much out of the concerns of *Why History?* it ought to be noted that it also has certain similarities and intentions to *Rethinking History*. Now over ten years old and about to be published as a Routledge Classic,[6] *Rethinking History* sought to offer what was at the time a somewhat lonely, popularising critique of the then predominant ways of thinking about academic history, a situation which has at least in some ways changed. On the one hand, in the intervening years the number of books — including those offering further critical alternatives to existing historical orthodoxies — has much increased, and most undergraduate and postgraduate programmes now have courses that cover historiography, historical theories and methods, and historical philosophy. And on the other hand, it is undoubtedly the case that the intellectual level at which more recent works are pitched has become much more sophisticated and rigorous.

And yet, despite the acuity of these texts and their desire very often to bring to bear upon the old discipline of history poststructuralist, postfeminist, postmodern and other 'postist' ways of thinking in order to open up history to new voices and agendas, I've already noted that academic history remains in business, albeit limping somewhat. Consequently, in this book I try to take into account the changes that have taken place over the last decade. This has meant that, first, I have had to take on board the kind of critical theoretical work that has become more popular even though this may have affected the language and, possibly, the occasional difficulty of the present text. In a way this is a difficulty hard to avoid, but I have tried to make this work as accessible and as student-friendly as possible. And second, this book is written in the belief that new students of history need to be made aware of these present debates and of the exciting new directions they arguably herald. Like *Rethinking History* then (which this book by no means supersedes but rather tries to complement – for the issues which it addresses have by no means gone away) the present text is written in a purposefully polemical tone so as to be deliberately provocative. And, again like *Rethinking History*, it is a text that has been kept intentionally short with a minimum of scholarly apparatus so that it might be used as a convenient 'set-text' for courses on contemporary theoretical discussions.

My second introductory point is that all texts are obviously inter-textual; that is, they are dependent for their sense of sense on many other texts no matter how much one tries to say new things and so 'begin again'. And I want to acknowledge that this text is very much influenced by three writers and the theoretical ambience they have created for other people to work in: the already mentioned French theorist Jacques Derrida, the American theorist of history Hayden White, and his Dutch counterpart, Frank Ankersmit. I am, I think, a fairly critical person, but I find it difficult – whilst being aware of the various criticisms levelled against them – not to agree with most of what they say. And I agree with them not only because I find them brilliantly perceptive and endlessly suggestive, but because they wear their respective hearts where I think all hearts should be worn – on their sleeves. Of course I do not expect – if they were ever to read this text – that they would accept my own way of thinking about things for which they have nevertheless been in part responsible, nor to agree with the particular argument they have on occasion been brought in to support, or even that I have understood them. Yet, I have read them, and I think I have personally benefited from having done so. Whether these benefits are obvious, or are communicated here to others either adequately or persuasively, I am not at all sure, but I hope that, at least in small part, their goodness shines through.

Chapter 1

Opening time(s)

> The reconciliation of all antagonistic forms in the name of consensus or conviviality is the worst thing we can do. We must close down nothing. We must keep open the otherness of forms, the disparity between terms; we must keep open the irreducible.
>
> (Jean Baudrillard, *The Perfect Crime*)

Once upon a time, a time which still casts its shadow over us, it was held that there was something *intrinsically* important in various historicisations of the past which could act as the basis of real and worthwhile knowledge. Put very basically, that old belief in the intrinsic value of the past was made up of two main elements. First, it was held that one ought to study the past ('the before now') 'for its own sake' and 'on its own terms', as if history was able to yield up its own essential points and not merely be the occasion for articulating our own. And second, by virtue of this attitude, the histories which were written by professional academics about this past were conceived of as somehow waiting to be *found* in the past; to be respectfully discovered and faithfully brought back to us, interpreted admittedly, but discovered – like fragments of some pre-existing jigsaw – all the same. The quest for this historicised past conducted *via* a research method that mixed empiricism and documentarism with the ethics of objectivity, neutrality and truth-seeking, further compounded the myth of the intrinsic value of the knowledge gained as a result of the exhaustive professional and scholarly efforts expended to get it. Not to subscribe to these two mutually reinforcing shibboleths of history – 'for its own sake' and 'on its own terms' — it was argued, was at best to fall victim to all kinds of anachronisms, relativisms, scepticisms and contemporary ideological pressures, or, at worst, to succumb to the apparently disastrous 'logical conclusion' that anybody could say just anything they liked about the past. And this was not good scholarship in terms of painstaking, selfless enquiry, but merely ideological and political bias or self-aggrandisement.

Coming from a position which accepts that most things held by historians to be intrinsic (historical facts, structures, periods and meanings) are actually only extrinsic ascriptions, these kinds of scary 'logical conclusions' are ones I think we can accept with ease for reasons that I will illustrate throughout this chapter. For there really is nothing essentially *in* the past to prevent the exercise of endless interpretive freedom by historians; indeed, the only values to be derived from the historicisations of the past come from *outside* of the past and from *outside* the gate-keepered craft-practices of the professional historian — in other words are *extrinsic* values. And such extrinsicality, which knows of no logical limits or proper procedures, is thus an open invitation to radical uncertainty for ever. Here at last we seem to have come to the end of the restraining proprieties of the professional, academic genre of history as we have come to know it.

The fact that 'the past' can be read at will and is so very obviously undetermining in relation to its endless appropriations (one past — many histories) is to be both celebrated and put into practice. To have one past but innumerable 'takes' and 'spins' is a positive value when everybody can at last potentially author their own life and create their own intellectual and moral genealogy — their own subjectivities — with no authoritative or authoritarian historicised past that one has to defer to or even acknowledge — especially a historicised past that seems to ghost-write itself with only the slightest intervention of the shyly-retiring historian, the handservant of the past loyal to his or her calling. For it is patently obvious that it is historians who create history and that 'the past' which they carve-up into meaning is utterly promiscuous. The past has and always will go with anybody without a trace of jealousy or a hint of permanent fidelity to any particular caller: hagiographers, antiquarians, professionals, Marxists, Annalists, Structuralists, fascists, feminists, pragmatic neo-Rankeans, anybody can have it. And why not? Nobody has a patent on 'the past'; it can be used or ignored by everyone. And why is this? Because the so-called past (the before now) doesn't exist 'meaningfully' prior to the efforts of historians to impose upon it a structure or form; 'the before now' is utterly shapeless and knows of no significance of its own either in terms of its whole or its parts before it is 'figured out' by us. Consequently, no historian or anyone else acting as if they were a historian ever returns from his or her trip to 'the past' without precisely the historicisation they wanted to get; no one ever comes back surprised or empty-handed from that destination.

There are no empty-handed historians because there are no empty-headed ones: the historicised past is always only ever us – back there. This is not as obvious to students of history as it should be; indeed, most professional historians consciously or semi-consciously disavow their *always* present-centred practices as they strive to achieve the 'history narrator as nobody' effect. Few have unmasked this particular sleight-of-hand – (which enables historians to continue to give the impression that they produce 'objective' histories in what approximates to a state of socio-political weightlessness) – better than Michel de Certeau, who puts matters thus:

> What peculiar kind of sustained, permanent ambiguity is it that historians practise … by which a 'real' past is taken for granted, another 'real' past is represented in texts, and a 'real' present is effaced from their production … The operation in question is rather *sly* … [for] the 'real' as represented by historiography does not correspond to the 'real' that determined its production. … The discourse [thus] gives itself credibility in the name of the 'reality' it is supposed to represent but this authorised appearance of the 'real' serves precisely to camouflage the very practice which in fact determines it. Representation thus disguises the praxis that organises it. [1]

If, as de Certeau is arguing here, all history is really historiography (the accumulation of the writings that make up our representations and presentations of the past) and is always self-referencing in terms of its own credibility, then it seems that the best way to keep in mind the

always present-centred figurings of the 'past' into history (for to claim
in the present that you should not be present-centred is no less a
present-centred claim than the claim that you should) is to go along
with Nietzsche's observation that the historian is, inescapably, *always
part of the picture of the historical past he or she paints*. And there is no
need to worry about this radical subjectivity, nor about the collapse of
the old subject-object distinction so central to western philosophy and
culture. For surely we are all now mature enough to recognise that
what passes for 'objectivity' is only ever us 'subjects', objectifying. As
Alain Robbe-Grillet cogently observes, this should not be seen as a
problem:

> Why ... should this be grounds for pessimism. Is it so distressing to
> learn that one's own view is only one's own view or that every
> project(ion) is an invention? Obviously I am concerned, in any
> case, only with the world as my point of view orientates it: I shall
> never know any other. The relative subjectivity of my sense of sight
> serves me precisely to define *my situation in the world*. I simply
> keep myself from helping to make this situation a servitude.[2]

We cannot escape the inevitability of our own subjectivity then – we can
only ever see the world from our own 'subject in formation' perspective.
But as Elizabeth Ermarth (commenting on Robbe-Grillet) suggests, this
is nothing to worry about; it is this kind of postmodern self-
consciousness in which we recognise and become aware of our own
radical subjectivity that prevents us 'from helping to make this situation
a servitude'. In other words, engaging with our own subjectivity,
defining our own 'situation in the world', requires a constant question-
ing and probing of our own assumptions and values. In turn the
production of this sense of critical self-distance (at times an almost
out-of-body experience) encourages endless imaginings and rethinkings
of what our personal and political identities might be. With some
confidence – which I share – Ermarth concludes that, today, we no
longer need an objective world to guarantee relations between one
consciousness and another or to guarantee an identity between
illusions. For 'there is only subjectivity ... only illusions' she writes,
which can only constitute momentary realities: 'The postmodern

moment comes in negotiating the transition from one [such] moment to another'.³ None of this is to say there are no 'criteria' for judgements and/or that we must therefore accept that everyone else's discursive 'reality' and historical constructs are all *equally* correct or all *equally* wrong. This is the supposedly knock-down argument so beloved of modernist historians as they raise the spectre of some looming ethical nihilism and consequent barbarism. For although there is no *ultimate*, objective foundation for our historical positions (or our moral decisions), we do still make decisions on the basis of preferences according to the tools at hand in any given social formation, we do still put worlds under descriptions, and we are still able to give (relative to such descriptions) argumentative support for them to those who might decide to listen to it and engage in conversation. And this has always been the actual situation. In that sense, nothing has changed. Apart from everything of course. For we are now fully aware that we have to live with an intellectual outlook where truth and objectivity, neutrality and disinterest, are simply agreements produced in conversations which are always between interested parties and within and against which we do have to make ultimately groundless decisions. By which process of thinking we arrive neatly at Jacques Derrida's formulation of 'the undecidability of the decision' (to be discussed further later on); a condition in which a decision has unavoidably to be taken (for even to refuse to make a decision is still a decision) but taken without certainty and 'subject' to endless revision. This is a condition of *logical openness* which also happens to be – for it keeps decisions always in a state of play, defying definitive closure – 'a good thing'.⁴

It is into this conversational/discursive condition that any intervention – a book, an article, a film, a novel – will make its noticeable or not so noticeable mark; beyond the reach of authorial intent, open for endless readings, and there for the relative taking or leaving. And the intervention of this book is no different. So, to the question of why still bother to historicise the past today and how best to do it, the answer which I register at this point is that I hope that a certain way of thinking may help allow the kind of emancipatory, radical politics essayed by Ernesto Laclau and others to enter the world, a politics of emancipation Derrida has also decided – as a citizen if not as a philosopher – never to abandon.[5] Especially now. For never before on the face of the earth, he writes,

> ... have violence, inequality, exclusion, famine and economic oppression affected so many human beings in the history of the world and of humanity. Let us never forget this obvious, macroscopic fact, made up of innumerable, singular sights of suffering: no degree of progress allows one to ignore the fact that never before in absolute figures, have so many men, women and children been subjugated, starved or exterminated on the Earth.[6]

My reason for still bothering with history thus revolves around a calculation of the degree to which the historicised past must escape all and every closure; must escape the closures of assumed objectivity and truth in the cause of personal and social freedom and of justice to come. And yet here, perhaps in its most mundane (or banal) expression, a question arises from the preoccupations of the mainstream professional historian which is ubiquitous in its presence and so may have already occurred to you. I would like to address it now so that I can get it out of the way before beginning to argue my case at length.

The question is this. If it is (the really rather obvious) case that there can never be a 'true interpretation of the past as history'; if it is very clear that you can never achieve a total and sufficient account of anything; if the impossibility of ever getting a definitive synopsis is begrudgingly *accepted* today as common-sense by just about every historian who thinks about it, then why on earth do people (like postmodernists) feel the need to keep going on about it? Historians are not stupid; surely they know all this? Are they not all at least liberally minded pluralists happy with numerous interpretations/interpretive differences? Is it not the case that many if not all of the positions associated with postmodernism – the various crises of legitimation, the absurdity of grand narratives, the acknowledgement of ambivalent and multiple readings, the overlapping of linguistic games with shifting rules and players, and so on and so forth – surely all these things and more, are now part of the weft and weave of everyday intellectual life? As is the much more grudging acknowledgement (or at least consideration) that relativism, perspectivism and ethical/moral undecidability 'go all the way down'. In this sense, are we not all postmodernists now?

To which I think the answer is, well no, actually we are not. I do not think that historians have given up on objectivity and truth; on the desire to make history a discourse truth statements are variously applicable to: an epistemology. These intentions may well be qualified nowadays but they have not been given up. And I do not think historians have all become happy relativists either. They should have done but they have not. Most professional historians remain stubbornly 'modernist'; that is, they remain intent on producing substantiated, empirically detailed and well-researched accounts in the name of accuracy and balanced, meticulous scholarship. And I think there are at least three good reasons for saying this is still the general situation.

First, whilst we may all be pluralists now, this does not mean we are all postmodernists. Postmodernism and pluralism are not the same thing at all; the former is not reducible to the latter. This type of reductionism attempts to slough off the 'extremes' of postmodernism so as to make it reassuringly familiar. Yet it misses the point entirely, for postmodernism *is* its extremes, *is* all that modernity cannot be compatible with. What postmodernism does to history – as Lyotard has pointed out – is to undercut the *form* as well as the *content* of discourse.[7] So what does this statement mean?

Well – problematising the *content* of the historicised past and various aspects of it – say for example, providing multiple readings of the French Revolution – is now par for the course. Obviously. However, nothing could be more ill-informed than professional historians who think they are 'postmodern' just because they accept multi-levelled perspectives; nothing could be more uncomprehending than to think that multi-interpretation is 'all postmodernism is about' and that, this accepted, then it is back to business as usual. For it is not. No, what postmodernists problematise is not the *content* of history so much as the status of its *form*. No matter how well formulated the *form* of history might be – its method, shape and structure – we can *never* show a definitive example of it. Thus, whilst many professional historians still retain the comforting thought (comforting because it sets limits/boundaries as to what can count as 'proper history') that multiple readings regarding the *content* of their discourse can at least be lived with because they remain within the *form* of a familiar history ('at least they're all historical'; 'at least they all respect the evidence'), the problematisation of the *form* of history takes this reassurance away. Consequently, it is now impossible to *ever* say what history really is (so that the query famously posited by E. H. Carr – what *is* history? – cannot ever be answered definitively) nor, by extension, what history's proper methodological procedures are. This is alarming for most professional historians of course, for if nothing is 'proper' any more then logically anything goes. Few professional historians, no matter how liberal and open to 'interpretation', can accept that interpretation – the interminable undecidability of history *per se*.

Second, *insofar* as our social formation is one of liberal, pluralist, modernist toleration, then that qualifying *insofar* registers 'the fact' that this is very much a social formation of arbitrary and always somehow hurtful closures. All social formations to be 'social' have to exclude, it is just that ours is one that tends to think of itself as an exception to the rule, one that prides itself on its liberal pluralism, its inclusiveness and hence its toleration. But this is partly a delusion, and a 'return' to even more repressive closures – of a radical intolerance – is a constant danger. Indeed, we might say that ours is *currently* a *recovering* social formation. Just as, for example, a once alcoholic is always a 'recovering alcoholic' – with all the dangers of a relapse into the previous addictive condition – so our social formation is a 'recovering sexist', a 'recovering racist', a 'recovering homophobic', a 'recovering xenophobic' social formation: relapse is always possible. And indeed, even this reading is far too generous for those who remain on the receiving end not just of previous but continuing – and *multiple* – manifestations of injustices; of as yet only partial recoveries. Moreover, and widening this out again, Derrida's invocation of the absolute enormity of global subjugation and pain in his *Spectres of Marx* is not about another 'globe' or another time but about this globe and this time. *Historians should have something to say about this*, but all-too-often their putative values of objectivity, neutrality, detachment, non-worldly 'academic' scholarship and specialised erudition about some aspect not of the now but of the past, become alibis for silence. With much justice Sande Cohen can thus argue that 'proper' academic history can best be seen as a 'reactive' part of bourgeois culture. For Cohen, historians tend to locate what is happening in the non-narrative present actuality (subjugation and misery are not narratives) in a longer, contextualising narrative form, as if to understand what is happening now you have to analyse not the present but what preceded it. But this really is an odd sort of displacement which promises to explain the now by *never* examining it. The frequent justification for the study of history – that it helps us to understand the way the world now is – is in fact one of its very hollowest. And as for changing the world...[8]

Third – and this argument is a preoccupation not just of Derrida but many others including Jean Baudrillard, J. F. Lyotard, Michel Foucault and Ernesto Laclau and is one I shall be developing at length later – any social formation (and in particular our technical, cybernetic, capitalist social formation with a vengeance) inevitably attempts to reproduce itself in as stable a condition as possible so that all potentially destabilising and thus dangerous excesses are either absorbed or rigorously excluded. This is the process of hegemonic social repro-duction and attempted closure which Baudrillard has described as 'the perfect crime', which, were it to be achieved, would be so perfect that no-one would ever know that it was taking place as it quietly folds unwanted phenomena such as difference, otherness and the excess – all that cannot be digested by current social and political formations – into the old and the familiar without remainder, without any 'loose ends'.[9] In this social formation – which Baudrillard argues against throughout his works – future events would not take place, not in the sense that things would not happen but in the sense that they would not disturb; all future shocks would be absorbed and the threat of their possibly radical alterity neutralised. Here the future would be preprogrammed into the status quo to ensure a desired continuity and so 'permit' a controllable flow from the past through the present into the future. All of which means – *and this is the point I want to make* – that for the past to link up with and support the ongoing present and its expectant future, then one could not and cannot – just cannot – allow the past to be read 'any way you like' by just anybody. By extremists; by non-historians. For the past, if it is to help ensure the reproduction of the status quo within acceptable limits (within those famous 'liberal

tolerances') cannot be totally open so as to allow innumerable inheritances, abnormal genealogies, interminable idiosyncratic figurings and
refigurings and 'lessons' to suit all and every occasion – this is far too
risky. No, what is required are proper, responsible, academic histories
(historians) operating within acceptable limits and armed with all the
usual gate-keeping paraphernalia: academic standards, publication
controls, peer reviews, benchmarks, responsible and efficient methods
and, in the wings, latent, ostracising power. That most academic
historians do not think of things this way is due precisely to the silent
and hidden mechanisms of ideological power in our current social
formations that simultaneously permit us to operate within such limits
whilst hiding them from us; the complicity is all so beautifully innocent
– ideologically speaking.

And so, in the name of a future which will hopefully not be a
reproduction of the same, that will run out of control; in the name of a
future that is open to strange, wondrous, disrespectful and disobedient
workings, I hope that the umbilical cord that intravenously feeds the
past, present and future with the sustaining power of the status quo,
can be cut in order to allow for new births. The very best reason I can
finally think of for saying that we may still need to have generous, open
histories which are both highly reflexive and explicitly emancipatory, is
that they might just help to prise open the attempted closures of
modernist historical thinking for the benefit of those who have still
not yet managed to get out of it.

In praise of excess – using Derrida

> I come now to our last theme, decision, without which indeed there
> would be neither responsibility nor ethics, neither rights nor
> politics ... A decision, as its name indicates, must interrupt, cut,
> rend a continuity in the fabric as the ordinary course of history.
> To be free and responsible, it must do ... more than deploy or reveal
> a truth already potentially present ... I cannot decide except when
> this decision does more and other than manifest my possibilities,
> my power, my capacity-to-be. As paradoxical as it may seem, it is
> thus necessary for me to receive from the other ... the very decision
> whose responsibility I assume. What I decide for the other, he

decides as much for me, and this singular substitution ... seems at the same time impossible and necessary. This is the sole condition of the possibility of a decision worth its name, if ever there were such a thing: a strangely passive decision that does not in the least exonerate me of responsibility. Quite the opposite.

(Jacques Derrida, *Deconstructions: The Im-possible*)

Let me now begin to develop the above remarks at the first of the two levels I discussed in the Introduction: to illustrate how historical openness is logically assured, that closure can never be achieved, and that such openness can hopefully be developed in the name of an emancipatory radical democracy by refigurings of the past. And I want to do this by leaning heavily on Jacques Derrida, a Derrida generally ignored by historians and many philosophers of history – a situation I hope to help rectify whilst in pursuit of my own project.

Jacques Derrida is part of that extremely powerful way of thinking which emerged in France in the 1960s and which opposed the idea that 'full presence' or total knowledge could be accessed and fully known through language.[10] What Derrida and many of his fellow French thinkers were doing was showing amongst other things the impossibility of reducing the infinite possibilities of thinking about what history might be to the finite or to the knowable. What was being celebrated here was thus the (logical) impossibility of closing down radical thought by constraining it within familiar *figures*. Indeed, what Derrida was concerned with was the logical impossibility of the definitive closure of *anything* so that future newness, or as Derrida terms it the 'to come', 'the promise', 'the perhaps', 'the arriver', 'radical difference' or 'alterity', is welcomed as both 'a risk and a chance' – as an exciting possibility or adventure.

So how does Derrida – who I want to use here as arguably the best example of this particular strand of French thought – guarantee such openness? Let me answer this by working towards history from his views on language. This may seem an unlikely place to start from if the desire is to subvert history, but it is not. For if language is interminably unstable – if it cannot be definitively fixed and thus 'closed' – then every discourse, including history, built as they are on and with language, must be unstable and thus perpetually open too. Language is actually the obvious point to begin, after which I shall look in turn at Derrida and 'decisions', Derrida and 'reading', and then directly at the implication of all these things for history. I perhaps ought to point out, given the generally received wisdom that Derrida is an extremely difficult writer, that some of what follows in the next few pages may need extra concentration. But such effort is, I think, well worth it. One of the problems with historians is that they do not have the patience to work at understanding theorists and theory (in this case Derrida and his idea of deconstruction); they do not have the desire to see the relevance of the kinds of things Derrida is talking about to their practices. But this is to leave such practices uninfluenced by some of the most exciting and searching ideas currently in circulation. In one sense of course this neglect is understandable, in that historians may 'intuit' that his ideas fatally compromise so many of their assumptions. But not being such a historian myself, it is these ideas which I want to help 'raise to consciousness' here.

On language

Let me start by saying that if a word was meaningful 'in and for itself' it would be what is called a transcendental signifier, that is, a word whose meaning was both self evident (so that as soon as you heard it or saw it you would know what it definitely meant) and that its meaning would remain the same for everybody throughout space and time. But obviously we have no access to a signifier like that. Of course, historians will not be surprised at this; it is obvious, they will say, that words change their meaning relative to their historical context. And they are right. But this sort of view, expressed at this sort of level, is too general to catch what it is that Derrida is saying at the level of language (of linguistics), and so it is at this level – where ostensibly stable meanings are subverted 'logically' – that we must begin.[11]

Because no signifier, no word, is meaningful in and for itself, then, because no signifier's meaning is immediately obvious outside of all contexts, then signifiers necessarily get their specific meanings *relative to other signifiers*. Consequently, a signifier always needs what Derrida calls supplementing by another signifier or set of signifiers to become a concept – what Derrida calls a signified. For example, take the word

God. In order to explain what is meant by this particular signifier/ word, we would have to add to it (supplement it with) a lot of additional qualifying terms such as Father, redeemer, omnipotent, Saviour and so on, the problem being that there is not a logical or finite number of such terms (or adjectives or predicates) that can be used so as to make them all add up to, be identical with, the word God 'once and for all'. We can always get another term, another adjective, another predicate to qualify the subject of our attention – God. And if this is the case, if we can never close down every possible description of God, then the word's meaning always escapes us and so becomes logically open forever.

And Derrida wants to say that all words are more or less like the word God. For Derrida, meanings are thus constituted not by self-sufficient signs/words, but through the phenomenon he describes as *différance*. In this notion, a signifier like 'God' can, as we have seen, only get its never-fully-completed meaning *relative* to other signifiers (Father, saviour and so on); it always needs *supplementing* by another set of signifiers to become a meaningful concept. But because the relationship between any two signifiers is never automatically derived or fixed or uniformly patterned, then the potential meaning that occurs when signifiers are connected is always contingent, arbitrary and logically unstable. For there is no logical guarantee that next time the supplementary or qualifying predicates that come will be the same as those which arrived before, therefore future meanings are always logically open. Moreover, given that words and their meanings rarely come in isolation but are generally embedded in chains of signification (in sentences, paragraphs, pages and texts) then the meanings of words within these various con-texts cannot be relied upon to retain their meanings in a stable way. Here Derrida wants to argue that the second signifiers differ spatially and temporally from the first; that they are spatially laid out so that those qualifying terms always come late – we need time to read them. This space/time structure is universal and everywhere; even though terms are repeated they are always slightly different according to the words surrounding them – when you arrive at the same words in a new context after you have met them in a previous one, the meaning will not be exactly the same. With *différance*, then, there is no way of getting meaning into the world that you can be absolutely certain of forever. Language like history – to repeat – never repeats itself.

This is not to say that words and discourses are not, despite their interminable differences, *relatively stable* in practice. And indeed it is this seemingly fixed nature of meaning that often mistakenly makes people think that there is something essential *in* language ... so that, for example, some historians suppose there is something intrinsic in the name of history that exempts it from being given endlessly new meanings and connotations rather than seeing that 'history', like all concepts, is an 'empty signifier' (a point I shall explain fully in Chapter 2). So meaning of any sort/type can never be permanently stabilised for the reasons I have just explained. And what the deconstructive approach then does is to extend this 'principle' from the linguistic into the social realm, giving it a particular political currency and urgency. Deconstructionists try to show how our various social institutions, conventions, law-codes and political systems are all attempts to stabilise 'unstable and chaotic' social and cultural formations. According to Derrida, what a

> ... deconstructive point of view tries to show is, that ... conventions, institutions and consensus are stabilizations ... are stabilizations of something essentially unstable and chaotic. Thus, it becomes necessary to stabilize precisely because stability is not natural; it is because there is instability that stabilization becomes necessary. Now, this chaos and instability ... is at ... the same time ... a chance, a chance to change, to destabilize. If there were continual stability, there would be no need for politics, and it is to the extent that stability is not natural, essential or substantial, that politics exist and ethics is possible. Chaos is at once a risk and a chance, and it is here that the possible and the impossible cross each other.[12]

So, as Derrida observes, the 'natural' chaos and instability of our social condition/circumstances is not a bad thing at all – for it contains within it the chance of new things to come, a chance to change things, to destabilise those stabilising systems that help legitimate existing misery and pain/suffering. So Derrida links the provisionality and openness of language directly to the future of radical democracy[13] – a permanent opening up of politics to *time* which questions any necessity of looking back to what has happened before: *we really can begin again.* Thus it is at this point that the past – the historicised past – enters into Derrida's thought as something which, although we cannot escape it fully, is something to make decisions about in the light of the present and the future, not for history's sake (as if history really had a sake, an intention of its own that we have to respect) but ours. Only we can decide – as best we can – if and when the past matters.

On decisions

It is at this point that we arrive at Derrida's idea of the decision; at his idea of what he calls 'the undecidability of the decision'. Again, and to reiterate, this is a crucial part of Derrida's arguments as he seeks to destabilise meanings (so that as we have just seen, new meanings can enter the world not least for political reasons) and to make us think, always, of the necessity to imagine in new ways rather than just rethink the old. Derrida's writing on his meaning of 'decision' is, again, complex. But simplifying massively I think I can get to what Derrida is driving at if I approach his idea via his discussion of justice.

Probably the easiest way to understand Derrida's notion of justice is to begin with the maxim that 'nothing repeats itself exactly' – and for our purposes here, especially not history. All decision-making situations are unavoidably new and distinctive, and any attempt to ensure that justice is done will not be served by merely reapplying previous decisions or laws, no matter how similar the circumstances. For if one refers back to, say, a previously worked out decision (or ethical system or law code) and merely applies it to a different situation; that is, if the decision that is made is merely the reapplication of a *previous* rule or formula, then no decision has been made at all, only an administrative act, which in turn means that justice cannot be done to the new situation in all its radical singularity; its uniqueness. All decisions thus lack sure foundations and are ultimately arbitrary – undecidable – this is what Derrida calls the *'aporia'*; the moment of undecidability through which one must pass when making a 'real' decision. Ironically, then, and against those who would tell you that learning the lessons gleaned from 'history' and living within already constituted ethical systems are precisely what we *ought* to be doing, Derrida argues that to make a decision and make it for the first time such that justice is done to both the decision-making process (which must always be knowingly undecidable so that every decision is a kind of experiment or invention) *and* to the recipient of the decision (who must never be pre-judged, even if such pre-judgements are enshrined in the most revered law codes), then at the moment of the *aporia*, the decision, one must *never* look to the past. For if you fold the new and the different into the old and the same, then all the possibilities of newness are negated; are said 'no' to. And Derrida always tries to say yes – 'Yes, Come', for saying no to newness is to effect a closure and this is very precisely *injustice*.

Of course Derrida thinks that, actually, no one has ever made an entirely just decision. But that is the *aporia* again. We might want to make a pure decision but we never can; we are 'always in a text already'; always already situated and constrained by our past and what we have wittingly and unwittingly inherited from it. And yet, though strictly impossible, in the name of a notion of justice that resists total understanding, one ought to try to be as free from one's inheritance as circumstances permit so that the least *violent* decision is enacted upon the other who is on the receiving end of it.

Moreover, it is the 'other' (this is the gist of the long extract from Derrida which heads this section) – the one who is affected in all his/her singularity by the decision – who will be the judge as to whether justice has been done to them and their unique circumstances. Derrida's ethical decision is thus never the simple expression of liberal individualism (free-choice-ism), for if it were then it would just be the incorporation of the other into one's own value system irrespective of theirs; the reduction of 'the other' to 'me', the reduction of the interest of justice to 'my' interests. No. For Derrida it is the other who will decide if what is done to them is just or not; they will tell me (as 'the other in me') if I am just; if I am ethical/moral. And of course that judgement by the other in me – their decision – cannot ever be perfect either, simply because he or she cannot totally escape their inheritance any more than I can mine. But nevertheless, the very idea of this impossible justice is the condition of the possibility of our efforts to think of justice 'justly' at all. And it is this *aporia* – that we must try to think in singularities if justice is to be done and yet we can never do it – that *logically* guarantees that every decision will always be, more or less, an act of necessary arbitrariness (or 'violence' as Derrida describes it). And so we reach another of these paradoxical *aporias*; there is no justice/ethics without arbitrariness or violence and with regard to this violence, no way of knowing, for sure, its extent. And Derrida likes all of this; likes the fact that we will always be a little in the dark; that at the heart of things lies a secret; that we will always get things wrong; here failure is not avoided or denied, but valorised. For Derrida the structure of the *aporia* therefore ensures radical doubt for ever and thus guarantees the impossibility of any total answer and, hopefully, total(itarian) certainties; here freedom lies in failure.

On reading

It is this idea of radical doubt, this idea of freedom through creative failure, this idea that we can decide which way to read things, that underlies Derrida's idea of what 'reading' ought to be. And again this is important. For if the past has to be 'read' to be understood (which it does), indeed, if it is the very act of reading which makes the past historical, which constitutes 'the past as history', then we can say that we both can and must read the past as a text or, more accurately, *as if* it were a text. For it is only textually that the past can be appropriated; can become the subject of our imagination.

This is not to say (as many critics of postmodernist approaches do) that the past is literally a text (a book, an article, a document and so on). Nobody (least of all Derrida) is saying, for example, that the Russian Revolution was just a text rather than an event, an actuality. Rather, what is being said is that it is only textually – as a piece of writing or another form of representation – that such an event can become the subject of our attention and our imagination. And I want to suggest that this requires that we read the historicised past as we read every-thing else, creatively and imaginatively of course, but also – whether we know it or not – unfaithfully, disobediently, between the lines. So what does it mean to read the past imaginatively? If, as the Derridean scholar Geoffrey Bennington argues, no text can compel an obligatory or necessary reading of itself – in fact it will always point beyond itself to another reading yet to come – does that mean that we can read a text in any way whatsoever? The answer is no.

For no text is open to any reading whatsoever; no text is absolutely indeterminate if one's comments are going to be about *that* text. Indeed, for Derrida, texts are always to be read *twice*; a first reading (a commentary or explication for example) which tries to be as faithful as possible to it, followed by a second reading whereby the text is subject to a series of interruptions which open up the various points of undecidability, moments of decision-making or *aporias*. In this way the text deconstructs itself through the tensions of its own fault-lines, its own interior inconsistencies; a deconstruction preparing it for an alternative reading it never intended to allow. Texts do not want to implode by virtue of their own *aporias* – but they cannot prevent this from happening. Consequently, it is this unintended freedom to read texts other-wise which actually – and this is the key point – constitutes a *reading* of them at all rather than a passive decipherment or commentary. Indeed, says Bennington, there couldn't be a 'reading' without this opening so that any reading, however respectful of the text being read, takes place and can only take place as an invention or act of disobedience in this space. This is why 'texts' are *not* messages and why classical theories of communication so beloved by most professional historians – who stress the need for texts to be clear, fully communicative, commonsensical and unambiguous – completely miss the point. For it is only when communication breaks down – when you 'just don't get it' – that the only meaningful acts of communication take place. It is only when – to make sense of it – you have *to rewrite* it for yourself, *figure* it out for yourself, that there is the chance of 'real' communication (real 'understanding') occurring. Consequently, for Derrida (and Bennington) the ethics – and thus the politics – of 'historical' reading, consists in negotiating the spaces opened up between the *faithful* first reading and the *unfaithful* second so that a degree of infidelity to any given text – *including the historicised past as a text* – is the constituent factor in reading. The ethics of reading suggest you have to try to get the text 'wrong' so as to open it up beyond its own attempted closures so as to make it yours. This is where things are turned on their head in relation to a normal, scholarly reading and the intentions of the text. For a scholarly reading tends to close down the internal inconsistencies and openings that allow a disrespectful reading in the name of 'faithfulness to the record', out of 'a respect for the voices of the past', and in an attempt to understand them 'on their own terms' so as to get them *right*. A deconstructionist reading is not so complicit.

On history

It is at this juncture that we arrive directly at history in two senses. The first sense, the first way that the above bears on history, is to see how there is always a series of decisions to be made as to what history is deemed to be and that, secondly, those ideas, being undecidable, leave the meanings of future histories open. And to make this point as strongly as possible, I want to say that there is always an unavoidable tension between what can be called the ideality of History (spelt with a capital H as if there really was a true History that transcended all empirical locations), and its actually always empirical grounding. What does all of this mean and how does it work? Well, let me start by claiming that operating here is what might be called in turn two guiding principles. The first is that to get meaning into the world through a discursive practice such as history there is always an unavoidable tension between any ideal concept (which Derrida calls the transcendental gesture) and its empirical or material inscription. That is to say – to begin to explain this – that although in every case the ideal concept of History is the motivation for its empirical working-out or elaboration, the empirical world is always unable to realise the full potential of the ideal. Thus History can never be fully present or fully known, its discursive practice always falls short of the desired 'ideal'. Paradoxically, then, the idea of history in its fullest sense is irreducible to any amount of empirical inscription, yet this is the only possible expression of it, the only way we can get the experience of thinking about it in the first place.

This leads to Derrida's second point, that the inter-relationship between the ideal and the empirical is characterised by an irremovable tension between them which Derrida once again calls *aporetic*, such that the creation of meaning carries within it the seed of its own deconstruction. Indeed, it is this unbridgeable gap, this permanent lack of total identity between ideality and the empirical, that is so crucial to Derrida. I am going to explain this further with an example, but first we might note that Derrida has a formula for expressing this tension which goes like this: that the condition of possibility for thinking (gesturing) towards History (and Politics, Ethics and so on), is simultaneously the condition of the impossibility of these ideas ever being able to find full realisation. So for instance, a historian like E. H. Carr in his book, *What is History?* thought that he could actually answer the question as to what history is by giving lots of concrete illustrations which, when put together, meant that you would have a definite idea of a history based on a sufficient number of material examples. Thus, Carr thought, for example, that history was a dialogue between the past and the present, and that with careful scrutiny of the past historians could demonstrate human progress and perhaps even project it into the future. But the problem here is that someone else could always come along (and they have) and give to the subject term 'history' lots of *different* characteristics or predicates and claim these as defining the subject 'history'. Accordingly, because we can never make the predicates or characteristics of anything (in this case 'history') equate to the ideal of 'History' once and for all and without remainder, we can never know what history really is.

Though we need the idea (ideality) of history to start thinking about history at all, then, the empirical manifestations we have to think such ideas through are never good enough – we can always get some more qualifying predicates. So that, living in the middle range between the ideal (the transcendental gesture) and the empirical, means that any decision made to try to fix a definitive meaning for history is always arbitrary, always inadequate. Located between two unstable poles (for the idea of History is really just a heuristic device as unfixed and contingent as the empirical), any decision as to what history is is ultimately an arbitrary choice along a spectrum which, stretching to infinity as spectrums do, is not a fixed decision at all but is rather eternally re-fixable; eternally refigurable. Yet even though failure is written into the very idea of History, we must, for meanings to be produced at all, decide for pragmatic purposes and on no sure foundations what we want the term to mean for us. Derrida talks here of the 'undecidability of the decision' as to what history and so on is, and will be. Here the future of the 'question of history' lies logically open, forever. And this logical openness is crucial for Derrida because he desires a future that welcomes what is to come in all its possibilities. Accordingly, the past – past politics, past ethics and the past *per se* – cannot determine the future in any logically entailed way and, argues Derrida, it ought not to do so; the present and the future is everything.

This is not to say that we can escape the past as such, 'the before now' as such, completely. But we can and we do always cut it up to suit ourselves. And indeed we may decide to so carve it up that it hardly exists; that it is, to use a phrase, 'very little – almost nothing'. But be that as it may, the point is that to inherit anything from the past necessarily involves a range of unavoidable selections, abridgements, appropriations, cuts and spins. To take just something from the plenitude of a 'full inheritance' involves endless and ultimately undecidable (aporetic) decisions. For as I explained at the beginning of this chapter, the past cannot tell historians which aspects of it 'it' wants them to study. The past contains nothing of intrinsic value, nothing we *have* to be loyal to, no facts we *have* to find, no truths we *have* to respect, no problems we *have* to solve, no projects we *have* to complete; it is we who decide these things *knowing* – and if we know anything we know this – that there are no grounds on which we can ever get such decisions right. As Bennington neatly observes, in the inevitable decisions that we have to make throughout our lives 'fidelity is always marked by, or tormented by, infidelity'. For Derrida then:

> The radical and necessary heterogeneity of an inheritance … is never fully gathered … Its presumed unity, if there is one, can only consist in the *injunction to reaffirm by choosing.* You must filter, select, criticise; you must sort out among several of the possibilities which inhabit the same injunction … in contradictory fashion around a secret. [For] if the legibility of a legacy was given, natural, transparent, univocal; if it did not simultaneously call for and defy interpretation, one could never inherit from it. One would be affected by it as by a cause – natural or genetic. One always inherits a secret which says: 'Read me, will you ever be up to it?'[14]

And the answer is that we are 'never up to it'. We can never know the exact status (truth) of that part of the whole we inherit, for we do not know the whole, the totality of history. Always partial and thus failed appropriations, inheritances are never 'full', never complete(d). The sifting out of that which is historically significant depends on us, so that what 'the past' means to us is always *our* task to 'figure out'; what we want our inheritance/history 'to be' is always waiting to be 'read' and written in the future like any other text: the past as history lies before us, not behind us. Derrida again:

> Inheritance is never a given; it is always a task. It remains before us ... 'To be' means to inherit. All questions about being ... are questions about inheritance. There is no backward-looking fervour in recalling this fact, no traditionalist flavour. [No] ... we are inheritors; the being we are is first of all our inheritances, like it or not, know it or not.[15]

The past is never (in that sense) over and done with, but is to be made tomorrow and the day after – and who knows what will happen tomorrow? The past is thus open to unstoppable newness; undecidable decisions and refigurings of a sort logically beyond any curtailment: anything can come; 'anything goes' – like it or not, know it or not. Even history's disappearance.

Resume/preparation

> Derrida is constantly alerting us to the constructedness of what we call the 'reality' of the 'extra-linguistic', and he is relentlessly, let us say, Socratically suspicious of the prestige of the ruling discourse, of the system of exclusions that is put in place when a language claims to be the language of reality itself [the past itself]; when a language is taken to be what being [the past] would say were it given a tongue.
>
> (John Caputo, *The Prayers and Fears of Jacques Derrida*)

Let me pull together some of the main points of this chapter and prepare the way for the next.

The reason I have used Derrida so much in the foregoing pages is that he, more than anyone else in my view, has yoked together the demonstration of the impossibility of linguistic/discursive closure with an emancipatory, political promise. Indeed, Derrida declares himself as having 'no tolerance for those who – deconstructionists or not – are ironical with regard to the grand discourse of emancipation'.[16] And it is in the name of this discourse that I have tried to show why and how we need to break out of the certainties of professional histories and re-figure the past, 'the before now', so as to inscribe within it an unavoidable and interminable uncertainty for ever. As stated in the Introduction, in Chapter 3 I attempt to sketch out a disposition which might allow us to imagine historians who no longer earnestly chant their mantra of anti-theory, objectivity, non-present-centredness and truth-at-the-end-of-enquiry spiced with just enough of that interpretive *frisson* that they like as they pretend to be so 'open-minded', but who welcome expectantly the non-foundational nature of all our figurings in every verb-tense (past, present, future) and their relativistic status. Contrary to what its critics may say, this is not an irresponsible position but one which arguably brings with it new moral responsibilities that are unavoidable; I have no alibis for any of the undecidable decisions I alone make in all my singularity.

But that is in Chapter 3, and between that and this first chapter lies Chapter 2. And that has its own contribution to make. For I am fairly sure that most professional historians will think that what I have said so far is pretty irrelevant to their everyday practices, if not totally irrelevant to them as human beings. Professionally speaking, at the level of the practice of history surely, they will say, the methodo-logical and other procedures of the 'guild' offer ways of closing down those reluctantly acknowledged gaps between the real and its representation/presentation which give rise to the possibility of a knowledge – an epistemology – that is still strong enough to bear that name. And I want to say that at the level of the meaning-ful historical text this is not a possibility. And so in the next chapter I look at some of the arguments which take away so many of the foundational presuppositions historians fall back upon when they try to justify their knowledge-making, epistemological ambitions. In this way I will argue that a history without foundations and thus made up of a series of arbitrary yet responsible decisions is precisely – if we need a history at all – all that we need: histories which are open invitations to that which has never yet been; histories which do not try to repeat themselves.

Chapter 2

Last order(s)

> Once across the threshold of postmodernity – and most of us have
> already crossed it here and there whether we like it or not – history
> in its traditional sense, along with its founding unitary subject, are
> no longer possible simply because the postmodern world is not one
> system but many. The discursive condition [of postmodernity] is
> not congenial to the One World Hypothesis, nor to the assumed
> value of neutrality, nor to the project of objectification with its
> emphasis on individual viewpoint and emergent form. With the
> recognition of postmodern complexities, neutrality and the rest of
> the values associated with history do not necessarily become lost,
> but neither can they remain universally applicable and, therefore,
> immune from choice or rejection. They are properties of some
> systems and not others, and the choices between them are vexed
> and difficult ones.
>
> (Elizabeth Ermarth, 'Beyond History'; *Rethinking History Journal*)

This chapter builds on the last one through six interconnected sections
all of which have the intention of clearing away many of the
presuppositions held by professional historians so that new refigurings
of 'the before now' can be made. The position I am arguing for should be
well established by now, but a reiteration of it in an idiom different from
the Derridean one used previously – a historical rather than a philosophical one – might serve to 'set up' this chapter as well as introduce
one of the two main 'resources' for it, Hayden White. For White's point
– that the insistence by academic historians that *their* stipulated
definition of history is *really history as such* is a hindrance to a much

more generous appreciation of the possibilities that lie dormant within
the term – supports the line of argument I will be developing over the
following pages. Thus White makes the 'setting the agenda' point that
there is obviously

> No such thing as a single correct view of any object of study but
> [rather] there are many ... views each requiring its own style of
> presentation. This [position allowing] us to therefore entertain
> seriously those creative 'distortions' offered by minds capable of
> looking at the past ... but with different affective and intellectual
> orientations. Then we should no longer expect that statements
> about a given epoch as a complex of events in the past 'corres-
> pond' to some pre-existent body of raw facts. For we should
> recognise that what constitutes the facts is the problem that the
> historian, like the artist, has tried to solve in the choice of
> metaphor by which he/she orders the world past, present and
> future.[1]

I On rigid designators and empty signifiers

> Freed from the author, the text too becomes an 'open sea', a space
> of 'manifestly relative significations no longer tricked out in the
> colours of an eternal nature' ... here the text becomes a *jouissant*
> affirmation of indeterminacy, a dance of the pen ...
> (Sean Burke, *The Death and Return of the Author*)

The first point to be made in this section will perhaps appear obvious
after the arguments of Chapter 1 but it needs insisting upon (and
perhaps again putting it in a more historical idiom than Derrida's) that
terms like 'the past' and 'history' which are so familiar to us in our
culture that their meanings appear natural, are not in fact natural at all
but the result of an always forced marriage between the subject term
(history) and its predicates (its characteristics). And this forced
marriage – and its implications and possibilities – can be fruitfully
illuminated through the use of two terms; namely, 'rigid designators'
and 'empty signifiers'. For what these two terms do is allow us to see
very clearly that no words, even familiar ones like the past and history,
have their meanings (their designations) rigidly fixed 'once and for all',

but rather that all words have the status of empty signifiers. That is to say, words can have new meanings attached to them that empty out existing meanings and refill them with different ones that can give rise, perhaps, to creative disorderings and un-namings; to the creative 'disrememberings of things past'. And all of this is important for us to recognise, for it alerts us to the fact that when we call everything that just happens to have happened before now 'the past' or 'history' (using these terms as synonymous in this instance) then, if we are not careful, we are already in danger of figuring 'the before now' in all too familiar ways which then trap us into a mindset that it is difficult to break out of. Thus, for example, to accept the words 'the past' and 'history' in the ways which are dominant in our culture is already to figure that which has merely occurred before now into a shape, a form, a unity and, quite often, a content, a direction and a significance; to objectify and thus to reify 'it' so as to give 'it' a life seemingly of its own which then makes demands on us; which holds us to account. And when this is done, then it suggests that the past/history really is a sort of containing object which we are somehow *in*: 'You can never get out of the/your past'; 'the past is both all around us and in us'. Which virtually rules out, by its powerful invocation of habitual common sense, the recognition that these *concepts* are just signs in search of an arbitrary (albeit in our culture, conventional) referent. This is not to deny, incidentally, that what happened before now actually happened. Indeed, this needs insisting upon. But the point is that these previous happenings were not in themselves 'the past' nor 'history'; they were just happenings. So I think it frees us up from being held in thrall to commonsensical rigid designations if we see that terms like 'the past' and 'history' are, like other terms, *empty signifiers*.[2]

This should be fairly clear, but a further comment on the notion of 'empty signifier' may be clarificatory in one aspect. For when I say that words are empty signifiers I do not mean that words are ever literally empty. Not at all; signifiers, including the so-called 'empty' ones, are *always full*. The idea of the empty signifier is not that signs or words are *empty* but that whatever meanings or predicates they are filled up with are arbitrary. What the idea of empty signifier draws attention to is that because the dominant predicate of every subject is simply the contingent filling up of a term as determined by those with the power to do so, then any designated 'content' can be *emptied out* and re-filled (or discarded or forgotten) by an equally contingent and thus never rigid/fixed re-designation – *ad infinitum*. Thus, in the case of those predicates which in common usage seem to be so obviously what the past/history is, it will be useful to use the term 'the before now' instead (as I have already done and will continue to do as contextually appropriate) so that their usually attributable predicates and their connotations do not stifle our imagination … all of this to allow us to indeed entertain exactly those 'creative distortions' Hayden White talks about.

2 But 'the past' is not history…

> Let's say that we manufacture a [linguistic] double of the world which substitutes itself for the world. We generate the confusion between the world and its double.
>
> (Jean Baudrillard, *Paroxysm*)

Salaried historians who make their living trafficking in history – generally in higher education – are usually proud to call themselves professionals, thereby distinguishing themselves from antiquarians and amateurs by dint of the predicates habitually attributed to 'professionals', such as rigorous methods, scholarship and erudition, so as to constitute a sort of club or a guild or, as Michael Roth has put it, 'a history tribe'.[3] Not anyone can be a professional historian. There are (as I mentioned in Chapter 1) qualificatory hurdles, peer appraisal, glass ceilings and all manner of excluding devices. But, once in, the insiders are generally ready to convince others, as they have by then invariably convinced themselves, that the history they 'do' really is worthwhile and that it really is history. And here I want to flag up the radically a-historical nature of that assumption. For whilst most professional historians do not for a minute hold to anything so vulgar as a Whig theory of progressive history, most actually *do* hold to a Whig view of historiography and methodology. That is to say, they think that earlier efforts made by previous historians to understand 'the before now' (although regarded at the time as being the doing of real history) have in fact always fallen short of that *really* proper history which, at last and by happy coincidence, historians today have actually achieved and to which previous gallant attempts can now be seen, in retrospect, as helpful, if benighted, intimations. But, of course, to the extent that historians today really do think that the genre of history they just happen to practise is identical to history *per se*, they are just confused. Nothing could be less 'historical' than the idea that the job description of today's professional historian is the embodiment of history as such and that that's it; that we have reached the perfected end of historiography; exhausted its potential. It is therefore more than a sobering thought to imagine that the summation of previous historians' efforts might find its highest form of expression in 'the nature of history' arguments as articulated by, for example, Arthur Marwick – it is a tragedy.

All of which is grist to Hayden White's point that any reflexive historian must be able to identify the ideological elements that underpin the particular history construct s/he works in rather than mistaking them for history as such. But as he observes, historians rarely consider the cultural determinants or function of their work. Rather,

> They enter the discipline. They do their work. When you point out to them that, 'Well, the kind of work you do presupposes or is based upon a number of implicit assumptions', they say, 'Well, I'm not concerned with that. I must continue to do my work'.[4]

And what exactly is that work? Again, White's point that what professional historians do is fundamentally not so much a method but a form of etiquette, strikes home. For the thing about the much-bandied-around term 'proper' history, he argues,

> ... is that it is, of course, a very British locution. The idea of propriety means that proper history is rather like proper deportment, it indicates an *etiquette* rather than a theory. I mean, proper history is the kind of thing that is done by the right people at the right time at the right place ... anyone who doesn't subscribe to the norms of professionalism is thus put down by saying this person isn't doing proper history.[5]

But it is not just that. For the persons, events, processes and structures of 'the before now', are the object of study by many other discourses of the human and social sciences and, indeed, the natural and physical sciences too. Not just historians but anyone – journalists, politicians, media commentators, film makers, artists – can and do successfully access 'the before now' often in ingenious ways which pay scant regard to the 'skills and methods' of the historian, skills and methods which White has characterised, on another occasion, as little more than the study of a language or two, a consideration of the works in his/her field to gain familiarity, sometime journeyman work in the archive whilst, for the rest, 'a general experience of human affairs, reading in peripheral fields, self-discipline and *Fitzfleisch* are all that is necessary. Anyone can meet these requirements fairly easily'.

Which raises the question as to why the professional historian is seemingly alone in being able to determine the proper answer to the question, 'what is history?'. And whilst we live in a social formation that prompts and then allows historians to talk endlessly about the application and assessment of 'historical skills', we might note in passing that such skills are not historical in any meaningful sense at all, but generic. 'Finding' and generating data, checking the provenance of sources/texts, reading critically, extrapolating 'evidentially', writing synoptically, these are hardly skills specific to history; think of the work of lawyers, geographers, literary critics or philosophers. In addition, there is something odd and slightly stupid about the very idea of 'historical skills' at all. For whilst we would not for a moment call the skills someone uses to investigate various aspects of, say, a desert island, 'desert island skills', yet it seems perfectly reasonable to some historians (there are whole undergraduate courses devoted to them) to call their applied skills 'historical skills' simply because the object of their investigation is 'history'. This is a simple category mistake whose mystificatory power we can all do without; there are really no such things as historical skills.

And whilst we are clearing the decks, we might as well get rid of the associated idea that the traces from 'the before now' which historians work on contain *in themselves* a specifically historical kind of information and that the 'knowledge' based upon it is a specifically historical kind of knowledge. Rather it is the application of the historian's particular discursive practices – the application of a 'historical' genre (rather than a geographical or a literary or a legal one; rather than a mythical, a legendary, or a fabular one) that *turns* such traces of 'the before now' into something historical; nothing is ever *intrinsically* historical – least of all 'the before now'. Thus it might be better to call such traces *archival* inasmuch as they can become the objects of enquiry of any number of discourses without belonging to any of them; historians have no exclusive rights to the archive; 'the past' does not in any way have the property of history *in* it. These are elementary points. But already they are helping us to get rid of some of the more common presuppositions of professional history. These are just the tip of the iceberg, however, so let us continue.

3 On significances to come

'Evaluation' in the aesthetic realm does not provide an equivalent to 'verification' in the scientific realm and a species of category error arises when [history] seeks to model itself on disciplines which proceed from axiomatic foundations. The meaning of a ... text does not equate to a mathematical equation: the choice between incompatible ... readings can only be made on the basis of aesthetic or ethical criteria.

(Sean Burke, *The Future of Biography*)

Even though historians are aware that strictly speaking it may not be possible to get rid of all their present-day assumptions and presuppositions that are, actually, the very things that allow them to think historically at all, most still try to do so. Most professionals still hold that the *aim* of history is, to recall, to understand the past on 'its own terms' and 'for its own sake' uninfluenced as much as humanly possible by their own 'historical context' for fear of committing the deadly sins of anachronism and distorting hindsight. For only by such an approach can a proper respect for the past be shown, a respect that the past will somehow appreciate and so be prepared to give up its secrets. And I want to say – along with Arthur Danto – that this aim can never be met and should not even be attempted in the first place if one wants to be thought of as a historian; to do what is being suggested here in the name of some kind of objective neutrality is precisely to do something which historians can never do. So how does this denial of normal, 'proper' history, work?

As Danto pointed out many years ago[6] – though his argument has obviously been ignored – the only conceivable representation of 'the before now' as it 'essentially was in and for itself' would be one produced by an *ideal chronicler*. Such a chronicler would be a person who knows about and who records absolutely everything that happens the moment it happens, who also knows the necessary and sufficient causes of such occurrences and their meanings, and who does so without any knowledge at all of the future – a position which, as Danto explains, 'would put the historian out of business'. For a history to be a history it necessarily involves a looking *back*. This immediately introduces hindsight and anachronism as unavoidable, *formal* requirements of history by even the most minimal definition (as a looking back at, and a presentation of, 'the before now'), all of which means that, ironically, the basic touchstone of the proper historian as s/he articulates it – to understand the past on its own terms and for its own sake *without* the benefit of hindsight – cannot ever be realised by a historian or indeed anyone else. Nor should it be. For the whole point of a historical consciousness is very precisely *not just to 'know'* the persons and events of 'the before now' as a contemporary might have done *then,* but as historians do *now*; looking back. Accordingly, the very thing professional historians seem to want is not only logically impossible but also plainly *anti-historical*.

This leads me on to my main discussion in this section which begins with the assertion that, in the light of the above, the only thing we can ever offer as a history is a present-centred *proposal*, a tentative *presentation* about how 'the before now' might be seen. In one of his many attempts to disturb our commonsensical intuitions about historical representation, Frank Ankersmit draws upon Jean Baudrillard's discussion of the tendency on the part of a religious believer to gradually eliminate God – the object of their devotion – and to recognise instead His presence in the images, icons or *simulacra* made of 'him'.[7] Thus, the believer who initially worships God through His image begins after a while to transfer his/her devotion to the images themselves – the simulacra – which were only ever meant to be a medium for the expression of God, the result being that we now have a condition where the image seems more real than the real; the image of God more real than God himself. Consequently, says Ankersmit, this way of thinking will 'inevitably render inapplicable and futile our traditional notions of truth and reference'. Why should this be so?

Well, for Ankersmit the one discourse where the thesis of the substitution of the image for the reality definitely 'possesses an immense plausibility' is history, not least because the once historical actuality is just as invisible to the eye as is God; we know Him (just as we know the past) only by their presentations. Thus we have no way of gaining access to the once historical actuality of the past except via our simulacra (our texts) such that we can say that, insofar as this once actuality has any life today, then it owes it entirely to the simulacra – the history – which historians have constructed of it: 'certainly in this case' Ankersmit concludes, 'we can say the simulacra precedes reality... that history is as much "made" as "found" – this coinciding with Hayden White's definition of history as 'a narrative discourse the content of which is as much imagined as found'.[8]

It is this argument which leads Ankersmit to his idea of histories as *proposals*; as presentations and not as re-presentations. And this change from representation to proposed presentation is to be preferred for two reasons. First, for a strong working definition of representation, the presence of an independently given historical actuality which can act as an independent check on saying anything (at the level of meaning; at the level of the text) is required. But if it is the presentation itself – the historians' text – which creates the reality to which it ostensibly refers in the very act of presenting it, then it is this presentation which creates past 'reality' in the first place. Thus the historian's narrative is not re-presenting the once actuality at all in the sense of presenting it *again*, but is actually presenting it for the first time whilst simultaneously proposing this presentation as a way of thinking about things as one of many such proposals – thus making it just another text amongst those which constitute the extant literature. Which means that, second, because *all* proposals can only be deemed relatively plausible *not* in relation to 'the past' as such but with regard to other historians' proposals or texts – that is intertextually – then when it comes to 'judging' historian's presentations/proposals *the past literally does not enter into it*; only texts matter historically. Consequently, we are free to make of the past what we will, without any kind of 'original past' that can count decisively to stop us. Few professional historians are happy with this freedom and many have tried to suggest repeatedly that there is still something in the past – what I want to call its *syntax*, its 'facts' – that prevents this kind of semantic or interpretive *laissez-faire*, this kind of semantic free-fall. But at the level of meaning, of interpretation; at the level of the text which is always more than the sum of its cognitive statements, the factual cannot hold out against the production of endless meanings such that semantic freedom well and truly runs its own unfettered course. So I turn now to syntax and semantics in that order to explain this further – a crucial explanation.

4 On syntax or the grammatical ordering of 'the before now'

> One challenge of poetics to history lies in the implication of the equation of representation and referentiality ... Normal, that is, traditional history, is shown to be but a conventional, hence arbitrary, mode of coding communication as factuality by presenting the representation as if it were entirely referential and realistic. The transmutation of so much – some would say all – of the referential side of history into the representational and narrative side destroys the effect of overall factual authority claimed for historical productions. Demystification of the historical enterprise, therefore, also delegitimises it as a discipline in this view.
>
> (Robert Berkhofer, *The Challenge of Poetics to (Normal) Historical Practice*)

One of the ways historians argue that interminable interpretive freedom can actually be checked is by recourse to the factual within history. These arguments take many forms but the common element in all of them is to say that certain things happened, traces of that happening remain or can be inferred, these traces can be used as sources for the establishment of fact-based evidence and that that evidence can then be used in arguments as pegs from which can be hung only certain conclusions, only certain sorts of significance and certain meanings. In this way it looks as if it is possible to pass from the evidential 'facts of the past' (syntax) to the significance and meaning of them (semantics); a move from facts to values (significances); from syntax to semantics.

But this passage is a logically impossible one. In the history of philosophy there has been no successful attempt – though many people have tried and some have indeed claimed success – to derive value(s) from fact(s) *logically*. This is not to say that we do not *seem* effortlessly to draw values from facts all the time in our everyday lives, but this is not what the philosophical argument is about. For although we routinely interconnect facts and values all the time we can never show a logical entailment from the one to the other; the fact-value argument is the argument that we can never logically draw from one fact, or one set of facts, one and only one value. For example, we might say that going to war hurts people and is therefore wrong; on the other hand we might say that even though it hurts people war can often be morally justified. Accordingly, if it is possible either to justify or not the act of war then it follows that there is no *necessary* entailment of values from the fact that war hurts people. Thus we are free to decide to draw (on undecidable grounds) whatever values, significance or meaning we like about facts (including the facts of the past, the present and the future). Until someone can show that there is a logical entailment – I doubt there is much chance of that happening – then we remain inescapably ethical, moral and historical relativists.

Facts, then, cannot stop interpretive flux; there is, as White has famously put it, 'an inexpungeable relativity in every [presentation] of historical phenomena'.[9] But as if this were not bad enough for the defenders of the faith, the so-called facts are themselves interpretive constructs as well. Consequently, the impact on history of the collapse of facts into interpretive phenomena further undercuts the use of facts as the basis for a resistance to semantic freedom, for interpretations are of course value judgements. This deserves attention for just a few more pages.

It is now nearly forty years since Roland Barthes in his *The Discourse of History* demonstrated that facts were linguistic entities.[10] For Barthes, historians perform a sort of magic whereby what is just a discursive concept – 'the facts' – are projected into a realm supposedly outside of discourse from which they can then be thought to *determine* the very discourse which posits them as facts in the first place. This is not to deny the actuality of past happenings, but only to argue that they do not count until they are given significance in discourse. It is discourse that makes the 'stuff' (the events) of the before now into facts ... and thus Berkhofer's comment at the head of this section that this collapse of the independent nature of 'the facts' to which the representation/presentation refers into representation and presentation destroys the effect of facticity claimed by most historians.

This may appear rather abstract, even irrelevant to the work of the historian. But of course it is not; it lies at the heart of every historian's meaning-making practices, as a short concretising extract from Chris Lorenz shows. For how is it possible, he asks,

> ... that with regard to an individual subject – National Socialism for instance – different historians keep referring to different states of affairs as facts and keep referring to different statements as true, and thus how is it possible that there is no guarantee of consensus in history? This fact is explained by the circumstance that factual statements and their truth value vary with their frames of description ... If we realise that what 'reality' looks like always depends on a form of description ... and therefore a perspective – it comes as no surprise that 'reality' cannot be used as an argument in favour of, or even for the 'necessarity' of, a particular perspective. [For] this presupposes a direct fit between reality and a specific linguistic framework [whereas] it is the other way round: it is the historian who tries to determine what the past 'really' looks like ... it is the historian, not the past, who does the dictating in history.[11]

Robert Berkhofer underlines Lorenz's point emphatically: the effect that professional historians *try* to achieve in their representations/presentations, he writes,

> Is the fusion of the structure of interpretation and factuality to impress the reader that the structure of interpretation *is* the structure of factuality ... rather than showing ... how the representation is structured to *look like* total factuality. The normal historian's job is to make it appear *as though* the structure of factuality had itself

determined the organisational structure of his or other accounts ... this is the illusion of realism.[12]

Hayden White has never had such an illusion; the only meaningful past reality for White is that produced by the shaping, meaning-making figure: 'figural realism'. This is a crucial way of reading and understanding things, and so let me briefly explain it. It helps to get rid of so many of the other presuppositions held by historians.

White takes it as axiomatic that histories – especially narrative histories (though probably all histories are narratives in their overall structures) are basically *fictive*. That is to say, though historians may wish to tell the truth and nothing but the truth about their objects of study and about that which they glean from the archive, they cannot narrate their findings without resort to figurative discourse. A literal account of what happened before now could produce only, at best, a massively abridged annal or chronicle of 'the before now' and never a history. For a history minimally requires – to be a history in any sense at all – a significant and meaningful organisation of the 'facts' which the facts themselves cannot ever fully provide. As a discourse about happenings no longer perceivable, historians must therefore perform two imaginative constructions. First, historians must construct their object of interest before they can, secondly, bring to bear upon it the kind of procedures they wish to use in order to explain and understand it within the genre (the kind of history they are writing) that they have chosen (their way of putting the object 'under a description'). This is the only way it can be ushered into meaning. Historical discourse is thus always characterised by a *double* presentation: of the object of interest *and* of the historians' thoughts about this object variously articulated. Consequently, as White comments, historiography

> ... cannot *not* operate the other functions which modern linguistics identifies as the different functions of the speech act: expressive (of the authors' values and interests), cognitive (of audiences' emotions, interests, prejudices), metalinguistic (seeking to clarify and justify its own terminology and explanatory procedures), phatic (establishing communication channels) and poetic (by which structure is transformed into sequence).[13]

Accordingly, it is the relationship between these elements (none of which come out of the past of course, but which act on the past's traces as they cure them up into meaning) which allows White to make the further point that such relationships are not only 'not historical' but that they are not fixed through some set of agreed methodological procedures either. In fact, the varying relations between these various functions are what White calls tropological; that is, the meanings which historians make are made through various types of figure – metaphor, metonymy, synecdoche and irony – it is these which produce the kinds of arrangements that the past is presented through. The connections between the people, events or situations presented in historical discourse, are therefore *not* logical connections but are metaphorical/allegorical. Further, since none of the discrete events which it is thought took place can be described as having in themselves an *inherent* arrangement or story-line (let alone some intrinsic value that is objectively there and which cannot be ignored), then the processes by which such inert phenomena are *turned* (troped) and emplotted into a narrative form they were never in has to be ... fictive. Hence, what 'realism' the narrative has must be that of the rhetorical figure – what else could it be? Which is why, at the level of the text, objectivity and truth, necessary correspondence or inherent coherence, drop out of the frame; history is not an epistemology.

There is no entailed passage from syntax to semantics then. All histories are inevitably troped, emplotted, figured-out and argued for from the historian's own position. Of course there are some historians who think that they can escape producing histories in the kinds of way White and Ankersmit have been suggesting, but this is not possible. The only historians who could escape this are those historians who do not trope, do not emplot, do not argue evidentially and do not do all of these things from an ideological position. No such creatures have ever been found and it beggars belief to think that they could possibly have been imagined.

5 On semantics

... Lacan's famous imperative 'do not give up on your desire', furnishes him with an abstract principle ... for to be thus faithful to the peculiarity of your desire first requires 'a radical repudiation of a certain idea of the good', that is, the repudiation of all merely *consensual* social norms ... in favour of an exceptional affirmation whose value cannot necessarily be proved ...

(Peter Hallward, Introduction to Alain Badiou's *Ethics*)

I want to base part of this section on some of the more original ideas of Frank Ankersmit and particularly his theories about 'statements and texts' and about 'narrative substances'. These are theories which shift our attention from the research/archival aspect of the historian's work to the shaping, figuring, aestheticising, textual and thus radically *semantic* aspects of historicisations of 'the before now'. These theories are outlined in many places and in great detail, not least in Ankersmit's *Narrative Logic* and *History and Tropology*, but the gist of his arguments can perhaps best be approached on this occasion via two shorter pieces, one of which appeared in the journal *History and Theory* and one which forms a chapter in his forthcoming book, *Historical Representation*.[14]

Turning to his work on 'statements and texts', then, Ankersmit argues that we can say about a historical text two things. First that such texts consist of many individual statements, most of which seemingly give an accurate or 'true' *description* of some state of affairs that existed in the past. These 'evidential' statements are 'found' in the 'historical' archive and have about them − when corroborated − the aura of facticity. This leads to Ankersmit's second point, which is that with the possible exceptions of some areas of the past with almost non-existent traces, the evidential traces and thus the evidential 'true' statements available to most historians allow them to write many more true statements about the historical past than are actually found in their texts. It is sometimes argued − it is a typical seminar topic − that there are no such things as historical facts as such, and this seems true in the sense that, as we have seen, 'facts' have to be given that status by much interpreting investigation or designation. But that investigation done, the result is not that there are then no facts but that there are millions of them. Consequently, the situation facing the historian is not one of non-existence or scarcity but of abundance. Accordingly, the historian's problem then becomes that of the selection, the distribution, the 'weighing up' and the giving of significance (which is never already there) always to just some of 'the facts' in always problematical combinations relative to – *relative to* – a whole range of interests which combine such facts in always ultimately indeterminate and thus arbitrary contexts. Thus, as Ankersmit says:

> Of all the statements historians could have made about the relevant parts of the past, they carefully select *qua* descriptive content and *qua* formulation, the statements they will ultimately decide to mention in their texts – one might thus say that the writing of the historical text requires of the historian a *politics* with regard to the statement, and that the *text* is the result of this *politics*.[15]

And the reason why, Ankersmit adds, historians are careful about their statements is that 'these statements, when considered together, determine the "picture" of that part of the past they wish to present to their readers as a *proposal* about how to figure that past'. And now we again see the problem of trying to verify as 'objective' or 'true' any resultant picture/presentation/proposal so produced, for such proposals (generally in narrative form) are of a different *kind* – not different *degree* but different *kind* – from singular statements such that their *proving* is an impossibility. For whilst it is the case – to recall – that individual statements of a *cognitive* kind can indeed be checked (albeit *relative* to the way they have been put under a description) against a discrete evidential trace to see if they *correspond*, proposals about the past can never be so checked simply because the past does not have *in* it prior proposals of its own for any later combination to be checked against, to correspond to. And since, Ankersmit argues, what is most crucial in the writing of historians is to be found not at the level of the individual statement but at the level of the proposed textual presenta- tion – in that it is these which stimulate historiographical debate and thus determine over time the ways we come to *imagine* the historicised past – then I think we have to concur again with his (and Hayden White's) point that 'history' is always as much *invented/imagined* (the combinations, the proposals, the presentation, the figures ...) as *found* (the facts ...), and that the resultant historicisations are 'inexpungeably relativistic' and aesthetic.

Ankersmit is then able to draw an important conclusion from this discussion about 'statements and texts'; namely, that saying *true* things about the past's traces at the level of the statement is easy – anybody can do that – but saying true things, cognitive things, about the past's traces at the level of the text is *categorically impossible* – nobody can do that. For texts are not cognitive, empirical, epistemological entities, but speculative, propositional invitations to *imagine* the past *ad infinitum* – Ankersmit again:

> If we take seriously the text and its *narrative substances* we will become postmodernists, if we see only the statement we will remain modernist. Or, to put it under a slogan: the statement is modernist, the text is postmodernist.[16]

So much for statements and texts. And as you will have noticed in the above quotation, Ankersmit has introduced the other 'concept' I want to talk about here; the idea of 'narrative substance'. So what are 'narrative substances' and how do they further help to subvert the epistemological status of historical discourse and thus keep histories open for endless refigurings and shapings; history not as an epistemology but as an aesthetic.

Perhaps the best way to get into this is via Ankersmit's discussion of W. V. O. Quine's classic 1951 article 'Two Dogmas of Empiricism'. In this article the two dogmas Quine queried were the empiricist belief in some fundamental cleavage between truths which are *analytic* – in other words truths true by definition independent of the facts (such as two plus two equals four) – and truths which are *synthetic* or precisely grounded in fact; in empirical actuality. And Quine's critique of this position was that there are true statements that actually fit into both of these categories, such that a combination of analytical and synthetic statements is absolutely *necessary* if meanings are to be produced at all. Consequently, this *necessary* combination of the analytical and the synthetic thus means, against empiricist objectors, that discourse *always* runs together synthetic statements about 'reality' and analytical statements arising self-referentially out of linguistic practices. Now, what exactly does all this mean for the status of historical knowledge, for it is admittedly a difficult point to get at first reading? Ankersmit gives several examples in his text to show the significance of what Quine is saying, from which I take just two here and add one of my own to try to illuminate its relevance.

Ankersmit's first example is Newton's law according to which force is defined as the product of mass and acceleration. Here we might say that the statement is empirically 'true' (a synthetic truth) because it is in agreement with the observed behaviour of physical objects. But we can also say that it is a conceptual/analytic truth (true by definition irrespective of the way the empirical world actually is) and thus 'not' of the world. And, for Ankersmit, Newton's law – its meaning – is paradigmatic of the way meaning *per se* gets *put* into the 'reality' of *our* world; namely, through the necessary use of both the non-worldly, imaginary analytical concepts of force, mass, acceleration, and the empirical (insofar as we understand the now 'empirical' to be the manifestation of previous usages/practices). And precisely because this necessary, analytical component is definitionally 'true' *irrespective* of the way the world is, then this act of the self-referential imagination means that meanings are, once again, as much imagined (the analytic) as found (the synthetic). Consequently, the point of this argument for historians is that, to the chagrin of the mainstream, empirical type, so-called historical knowledge can never just be of the cognitive, empirical, synthetic kind. The 'historical' evidence never fully *dictates* or necessarily *determines* the analytical categories by which it is invested with significance, so that, always a mixture of the imaginary and the actual made real via the mediations constituting reality effects, the empirical basis for historical knowledge – for objectivity and truth at the level of the text – collapses. History is *not* – and this needs to keep being repeated – an epistemology. Of course, says Ankersmit, one can see why historians are attracted to the idea that 'historical evidence' *does* dictate which presentation the historian should propose about the past. For only on this assumption could one run the argument (as Marwick or Evans do) that nothing of much interest happens in the journey from the evidence to the text. But of course this is completely wrong. As we have seen, in the historicising of the past – in the way it is figured, troped, shaped, narrated, etc. – *everything* happens as description becomes presentation and as the 'referent collapses into presentation', leaving us with the insoluble task of, in a nutshell, trying to tell where, precisely, *presentation ends and reality begins or where reality ends and presentation begins*; either way, an epistemology which *thinks* it can tell drops out of the frame; I mean, what is the answer to an *aporia* like this? All of this can now be very easily illustrated by a second example from Ankersmit to make the point unmissable. Think, he says, of a study of the Renaissance or the Enlightenment. Here, just as with the Newton example, such a study contains both the empirical/synthetic basis for a specific view of these 'phenomena' as well as a proposed definition of them. As Ankersmit puts it:

> Lots of historians have written books on the Renaissance stressing different aspects of the past and this is why they come up with different definitions of the Renaissance or the Enlightenment. And, if this is how they decide to define the Renaissance or Enlightenment, then all that they have been saying about it must be (analytically) true since what they have said about it can analytically be derived from the meaning they want to give to the terms Renaissance and Enlightenment. It is thus a conceptual 'truth', just as Newton's law can be interpreted as a conceptual 'truth'. Consequently, we cannot distinguish between truths *de dicto* and truths *de re*, and so the kind of criteria that are decisive for 'meaning' are not reducible to questions of truth or falsity. For here it is essentially a decision about which set of 'truths' we might prefer when we are looking for the best account of the relevant parts (for us) of the past. Here, truth is not the arbiter of the game, but its stake so to say.[17]

Let me now add an illustration of my own to underline Ankersmit's point. Let us take the 1960s in Britain. And let us say that a whole range of historians agree on its description and on what might be called the *facts* (the syntax) of the 60s. And then they have to address how to present the 1960s in terms of its significance, its meaning, its semantics. Was it, say, a decade of trauma or years of banality? Or Joy? Or was it *really* a lazy decade, a sort of snoozy-doozy decade, or was it, *really*, the Swinging Sixties? Here the way the events of the sixties were remain exactly the same – are synthetically/empirically finite – but the ways they are made into the stuff of meaning-ful historical narratives are infinite; I mean, how could you ever definitively *know* just by empirical work that the sixties really were swinging rather than snoozy? And hence, for Ankersmit, the substance of historical narratives (his *narrative substances*), are organised and thus constituted precisely through the use of such proper names as The Enlightenment, The Renaissance, The Swinging Sixties, The 17th Century Crisis, The Industrial Revolution, etc., conceptually, analytically, by definition irrespective of the actual conditions of the past. Ankersmit explains this in a really crucial paragraph which locates precisely the status *in* history of 'the past':

> Such notions as The Renaissance, etc, should thus be seen as the *analytical* names of narrative substances, and thus, as far as reference is concerned, they must be denied the capacity to refer to anything outside of the text: they refer *only* to *narrative substances*, that is, a set of statements contained by the text. For what prevents such narrative substances from referring outside of themselves is because the Renaissance, say, didn't actually exist to so refer to. Similarly, the Enlightenment is a concept performatively produced by *colligating* the text's *internal statements* and thus there is nothing outside them for them to refer to. Which means that narrative substances are only ever analytically 'true' *via* the texts' internal statements and never externally (synthetically) true because there is no Enlightenment 'out there' for them to correspond to *before* the narrative substance creates it as a collective/proper noun for *its* set of statements.[18]

Of course, concludes Ankersmit (and this is responsible for the way terms like 'The Renaissance' are sometimes held to refer to actuality), if a narrative substance becomes widely accepted by historians it sometimes looks *as if* there really was a Renaissance out there and it has been *discovered*. But all that is actually going on here is the widespread acceptance of a *proposed* way of thinking through an ultimately arbitrary analytical category; nothing else. From which position Ankersmit draws three specific conclusions.

First, because there is no past ever given to us *plain* against which we can compare differently *imagined* Renaissances to see which one *corresponds* to the past actuality *per se*, then the past *per se* has absolutely no role to play in historical discourse. From the point of view of historical knowledge, 'the past' is a useless notion. 'Historically speaking' texts as combinations of the synthetic and the analytic are all we have, and we can only compare texts against texts. Intertextuality – not the past *per se* – is, once again, the always problematic, interpretive, bottom line.

Second, Ankersmit draws attention to how historical reference is achieved through the application/ascription of *narrative substances*. And this is important to keep stressing. For while, when pushed, most historians will agree that there are no such things as narratives *in* the past, nevertheless, they will generally maintain (or work on the assumption) that 'the past' does have within it its own coherence and that this, at least, can be 'reflected'. And Ankersmit's point is that this is not so; that our histories reflect nothing – no unity of significance, no correspondence, no coherence; rather it is the historians' narratives that give coherence. For as soon as we go beyond the single statement to sets of statements, and then all the way up through tropings and emplotments and argumentative devices and ideological positions, any coherence in histories can be achieved only through the coherence of linguistic procedures. Historical *substance*, then, concludes Ankersmit, 'must not be conceived of as being part of historical [actuality] but as originating in language: the historian's *substance* is, therefore, a *narrative substance* and its coherence is *not* found but is *made* in and by his/her text'. Of course.

Third, the unending interpretive flux which results from this condition is an integral part of political freedom. For freedom to exist there must – as we saw in Chapter 1 – be choices, decisions, and thus permanent opportunities for such decisions. Accordingly, if there was only one interpretation of the past, then that would obviously no longer be an interpretation but *the* truth. And this would then have to be accepted save by those who would be happy to be dissenters – and be prepared to be treated accordingly. Here 'truth' begets closures of all kinds. Politically, then, it is not the laid-back relativists whom one needs to be afraid of but people, or institutions, or states, who claim to know the truth of things at the actually irreducible level of interpretation/appropriation. And so in this way the freedom of interminable interpretation/appropriation is once again seen as a 'good thing'; here we are indeed back to Derrida and the arguments of Chapter 1.

6 Experiencing 'the before now'

> A succession of objective advances *may* take us to a new
> conception of reality that leaves the personal or merely human
> perspective further and further behind. But if what we want to
> understand is the whole world, we can't forget about these subjec-
> tive starting points indefinitely; we and our personal perspectives
> belong to the world.
>
> (Thomas Nagel, *The View From Nowhere*)

I think that the above arguments – which underline again and again that
history is not an epistemology and that at the level of historical text
objectivity and truth do not come into it – are as compelling as
arguments can be. But such arguments raise the question of how, if we
still wish to do so, we might *experience* 'the before now' in any
meaningful sense. As it happens Ankersmit has written perceptively
on this area and so I want to summarise at this point just a little of what
he has to say before relating all of this back – by way of a non-Ankersmit
experiential story – to the whole theme of this book; my own story acts
as a sort of conclusion ...

According to Ankersmit, then, a historical proposal, a historical
presentation is essentially a substitute – *a thing* – which stands in as an
object in its own right in place of an actual or an absent object; thus, a
painting of a vase of flowers is a substitute for an actual vase of flowers,
a model of a horse for an actual horse. Similarly, because neither the past
nor its traces can present themselves as history, historians do it for them;
if 'the before now' is to enter – transformed – into our consciousness as a
history then, as we have seen, it has to do so by way of a textual substitution, a simulacrum. Which means that the phenomenon and the
presentation of it are in different categories of being. For a substitute is,
after all, never the actual, the 'real thing': a painting of a vase of flowers
just would not be a painting if it actually was a vase of flowers; a history
just would not be a history if it actually was 'the past', and this difference
is permanent, i.e. ontological; there is no way that the past as past can ever
itself be a history.

Now, Ankersmit sees at least two consequences flowing from this. In
the first place, while traditional notions of epistemology tie words to

things, a presentation ties things (in this instance the text is a thing) to things (in this instance 'the past'). Accordingly, the text is as much or indeed more of an object in the world than the 'thing' it depicts. Thus, at the level of the historical text it is never a case of comparing 'words to things' as traditional epistemology has it, but only of comparing 'things to things', and this can only be done *metaphorically* ... this object, this painting, *as if* it was a vase of flowers; this object, this text, *as if* it was 'the past' ... so that any questions asked about the knowledge status of such phenomena are, again, metaphorical and therefore figurative, shaping and so aesthetic questions (of style, of design). And second, because of the ontological gap between the object of our enquiry and the resultant artefact, between the past as such and the historical text, total precision, such as you might get when comparing words and things at the level of the singular statement, is unattainable. As Ankersmit puts it:

> Total precision can only be achieved if we have at our disposal some generally accepted standard or scheme determining how words are or ought to be related to things. But such epistemological standards or schemes will typically be absent in the case of representation ... at most each representation could be seen as a *proposal* for such a rule to be generally accepted.[19]

Presentation thus again takes us into the discourse of aesthetics: of pictures, gazes, looks, impressions, feelings, sentiments, desires, appreciations; of figuring and refiguring. And I believe, as Ankersmit does, that this is a good way of thinking about those imaginative, aestheticised artefacts we call history texts/books. For aesthetics frees us up to new ways of imagining.

And this allows me to make one more important point. Which is that there is, after all, something very literal about written texts which gives readers of them the strong impression that we can expect 'words' to be something we can get 'correct'. We expect words, and texts even, to be somehow right, accurate, even true. Yet we do not expect this from a painting. Imagine several painters – Gainsborough, Turner, Picasso, Warhol, Hockney – all painting the same two people against the same, scenic backdrop. Do we expect for a moment – indeed would we want them to be – identical? Of course not. What we expect and what we will always get are five very different presentations, all of which will be appropriate from the painter's individual 'point of view', which we recognise as the personal signature of each of them; they have their preferences. Similarly, if we were to ask five historians – Christopher Hill, Natalie Zemon Davis, Norman Stone, Cornel West, Simon Schama – to give their 'impressions' of, say, the French Revolution of 1789 based on one agreed set of traces, we would not expect for a moment that they would be the same. To be sure they will all be histories (just as the paintings will all be paintings) and so they will have the reassuring comfort of at least being that. But we can take that reassurance away by problematising the very *form* of history (as we saw in our Lyotard example in Chapter 1) leaving us to then depict 'the before now' in recognisable ways, or not, as desired.

At the end of his book *Metahistory*, Hayden White makes the same point. Placed as we are, he writes,

> Before the alternative visions that history's interpreters offer for our consideration, and without any … theoretical grounds for preferring one vision over another, we are drawn back to *moral and aesthetic* reasons for the choice of one version over another as the more 'realistic'. The aged Kant was right; in short, we are free to make of the past what we will … in whatever modality of consciousness is most consistent with [our] own moral and aesthetic aspiration.[20]

In effect, then, what makes all of us prefer one sort of historical consciousness – one way of seeing, gazing, reading, writing, being – over another, is one's *own* sense of sense, a sense gained from, in the end, our singular experiences.

Our own experiences. Experiencing 'the past'; the historicised 'before now'. How does that work? Clearly there is a sense in which one can re-call one's own life, one's own 'life time' (an interesting phrase deserving much attention) but even then, always imperfectly and in ways constantly revisable (for merely to think of one event and then to think of it again makes that event in the light of one's first thought about it different – *iterated*). So how do you experience 'the past'; the long ago 'before now' – say some aspect of 'Europe' in the thirteenth or the eighteenth century? And, of course, the answer to that question is to avoid thinking literally. For to talk about experiencing this kind of 'before now' is not to talk about experiencing the actual thirteenth or eighteenth centuries but their historiographical presence; the presence of the absent in texts, the only place it can be. And then the question, suitably displaced from past actuality to presently extant texts, is, how do you experience the various textual presentations such that you prefer one account, or set of accounts, over another, over the rest? And here your personal experience is all you have; for some reason or another you decide that you just like E. P. Thompson better than Geoffrey Elton, like Hayden White better than Richard Evans ... something connects. But what? And all I can say is that something in one's life, something in one's experiences, something ultimately undecidable to do with one's mood(s), disposition(s), dream(s), imagination, makes one like this rather than that; decide this way rather than that way.

There is nothing unusual in this. It is how we live our lives. So, to see how this works, let me draw a couple of analogies from what I suspect is not an unfamiliar situation to many people – the only thing you can do when no other explanation can be given ... 'think of things this way ...'.

Let us say, then, that you arrange to meet a person – let us say a woman – with whom you have recently fallen in love, at the front of the National Gallery in London. Let us say that she is late. In the time you have to wait – which seems an eternity but is only fifteen minutes (such is the 'moody' phenomenology of time) – maybe hundreds of people walk past. But who knows, you do not even see them. Something in your expectation – an expectation refracted through your previous experiences – blanks them out. These people are not for you though they may be for others; for others these are mothers, fathers, brothers, sisters, sons, daughters, lovers, enemies, colleagues, friends, the person next door. And if your experiences had been different one of these could have been the person you are waiting for. But they are not. And then you see her. Your experiences got it right; you would pick her out in any crowd in the world. And let us say that you have arranged to meet where you have because you intend to go around the National Gallery together. And let us say you do it. You have been around before but this is a totally new experience; you see things differently this time; she is with you. And so you look at the pictures. Again. Hundreds of them. Some of the finest pictures ever produced, technically brilliant, variously evocative, maybe masterpieces and, in a sense, all 'equally good'. But, as you leave the Gallery and talk about the pictures, you say that, actually you only really liked two or three of them; only a couple appealed. And, to be honest, only one really struck a chord. For some reason, you cannot quite put your finger on it, for you, today, only 'x' is memorable; it alone evoked the experience you wanted. You did not much see the rest. Maybe tomorrow, in different circumstances, 'it' would not 'appeal'. But the picture will not in a very actual sense have changed; you will have. And so it goes on, indefinitely. These experiences may include epistemological elements but cannot be reduced to them; may include cognitive elements but these are not decisive. No. In such cases as these there is no 'true truth', no 'objective objectivity', no 'neutral neutrality', no 'absolute absolute', no 'universal aesthetic' operating, only experiences: experiences distilled, shaped, figured, expressed, lived; only likings, only preferences. This is the bottom line, a line incapable of underwriting anything for sure but capable, nevertheless, of sustaining a unique, singular life.

So the aged Kant really was right; we are free enough to make of things what we will, to put things under signs which the very putting there makes sign-ificant. So, what kind of new things might the sign of history bear, what fresh significations might be suggested, what alternative refigurings are there for experiences which by no means come from nowhere but which are not so deeply entrenched that they are already too familiar; what might we be up for, people like us?

Chapter 3

Beginning again
On disobedient dispositions

> The hope of the [strong poet] who has found a way to describe that past that the past never knew, and thereby found a self which her precursors never knew was possible ... is that what the past tried to do to her she will succeed in doing to the past: to make the past itself, including these very causal processes which blindly impressed all her behavings, bear *her* impress. Success in that enterprise – the enterprise of saying 'Thus I willed it' to the past – is success in what Bloom calls 'giving birth to oneself'.
>
> (Richard Rorty, *Contingency, Irony, and Solidarity*)

I start with a one-paragraph resumé.

Think of a history which exists in the world of the proper, professional, academic historian firmly rooted in the intellectual milieu in which most are rooted, in the realm of 'the real'. Such a history – we should know it well by now – will be reassuringly and communicably realist, obviously, and also, I think, empiricist, factualist, objectivist and, with its privileging emphasis on *the* primary (and thus 'original' and thus 'authentic') sources, heavily documentarist. Such a history will be studied for the past's own sake and not ours. On the past's own terms and not ours. And thus non-anachronistically and disinterestedly as opposed to present-centred and ideologically (as if non-anachronistic histories were possible and as if disinterest were not yet just another position), the interpretive flux which persists even given these strictures to 'truth at the end of enquiry' being accommodated by passing it off as a sign of academic freedom in ways which strengthen notions of liberal openness (as if such toleration did not turn into an intolerant ideology when having to deal with those who challenge not just its putative content but its forms – at which point we meet the accusatory language of 'extremism'). And such a history will pride itself on its robust, no-nonsense language of transparency to communicate in a coherent and orderly manner the coherent and orderly 'before now', all this without fully realising that such coherence and order is there only by courtesy of the relative coherence of language as such which, when cured up into a meaning-ful narrative form gives that very same form – narrative – to the formlessness of 'the before now', the resultant *substance* of this literary production – history – thereby being constructed, structured and thus constituted linguistically. Such a history – a modernist history of the academic genre – will scarcely recognise itself as a product of such *narrative substances*, but it is, just as all histories are. And it is histories of misrecognition like these, that are arguably *passé*.

And so, let us think again. Let us begin again. And let us think this time in postmodern ways. Let us go with the idea that, if history is *just us back there*, throwing our voice, then that history, like any other history, will inevitably be constituted and understood by virtue of having the self-same characteristics by which we constitute and understand ourselves. And think now of the kind of characteristics we inhabitants of postmodernity – we postmodernist subjectivities in process – have, 'like it or not, know it or not'. And think of the possibilities this opens up for a refiguring of 'the before now' beyond modernist figures.

Thus (and this goes back to my opening remarks about 'subjects in process' in the Introduction) such 'subjects' will see themselves as constituted performatively so that they are constantly being made and re-made, read and re-read, written and re-written, incessantly and interminably. Such subjects will see themselves as always temporally and spatially positioned and repositioned yet, lacking any fixing, foundational anchor, intrinsic nature or inner meaning, knowable purpose or destiny, then, decentred and fragmented, the sometime product of a re-enactment of norms which are radically contingent, they will remain ultimate mysteries even to themselves. This is a some-time self held together in what can only be a fictional unity which, it is hoped, will enable enough coping practices to develop such that one can survive in ways deemed variously desirable.

Consequently, this is a self which will understand 'the before now' (just as it understands the present and the future) as sometime appropriable and copable with by virtue of these self-same features. So that 'the before now' is regarded as unattainable in its whole and relativistic in its parts, as endlessly readable and re-readable, writable and re-writable; as demonstrably contingent and serendipitous, and so of a kind that can only be given a historical shape or a style or a meaning (a figure) via a series of interpretive, perspectival decisions which are ultimately undecidable (here we meet, again, inescapably, the Derridean 'undecidability of the decision') so as to produce some kind of unity that is clearly a fictional fix, an act of the imagination; indeed, as something clearly *fabular*; that is to say, as something which is told, narrated, having no 'real' existence outside of the tale, of the telling. As a product that is, quite literally, self-referencing.

And now think of this 'self' in a positive, optimistic way, through the idea of the 'outsider'. That is to say, think of this kind of self as an *intellectual* self who runs the kind of uncompromising critique of the inside, the status quo, which Edward Said in his *Representations of the Intellectual* argues just *is* the role of the intellectual. For Said, the intellectual is a particular kind of person. A person endowed with the capacity for representing and articulating a hopeful, uncompromising, emancipatory message. A person whose works have a radical, sustained cutting-edge. A person happy to raise embarrassing questions, not to take 'no' for an answer, relentlessly confront dogma and orthodoxy and keep in focus 'those people and issues that are continually forgotten or swept under the rug'.[1] This is a person who enjoys never being fully adjusted, of existing beyond the chatty, inconsequential 'reality' inhabited by the natives, of remaining immune to accommodation; an unco-optable, *disobedient* person. And this is a person who not only accepts the fate invariably meted out by various establishments to this thorn in the flesh − the status of the relative *exile* − but who also welcomes it. Who likes being marginal. Who accepts that his or her awkwardness, 'eccentric angles of vision' and unwillingness to follow established paths, gives a freedom and integrity that makes him or her beholden to no one and is ready to accept the consequences of that position: that one can never be settled, never fully accepted, never be entirely comfortable, never 'be at home in one's home'; that one actually relishes being, as Rilke put it, 'a perpetual beginner in your circumstances'.[2] And think of this position as one which allows you to express your beliefs both within the narrower discourse you are primarily engaged in (history) and more generally, politically, and to connect these two things.

In his book *Ethics: An Essay on the Understanding of Evil*, Alain Badiou articulates a way of thinking which helps to make the occupation of this intellectual position an always positive one. For Badiou (not unexpectedly for a French thinker – though Badiou's own position is one he juxtaposes *against* Derrida, Levinas, *et al.*) it is necessary to think of the sphere of human action as divided between two very different but overlapping sub-spheres, the 'ordinary' realm of established interests and differences, of approved *knowledges* that serve to name, recognise and *place* consolidated identities, and an 'exceptional' realm of singular innovations 'which persist only through the militant proclamation of those rare individuals who constitute themselves as *the subjects* of a truth [an innovative position]; as the "militants" of their cause'.[3]

How does this militant occupation of a 'truth' (or as I read it here, this militant occupation of a reflexively held, innovative 'position') work; how can it be reached? Well, for Badiou, such an occupation can begin only with some sort of *break* with the 'ordinary' and the established by way of what he calls an *event*. Such an *event*, he says, has no verifiable content, its happening cannot be proved but only, in the light of our *experience* of it, grasped, affirmed and proclaimed; a new position which then persists by virtue of having an attitude of fidelity towards it, of commitment to it, a commitment which 'amounts to something like a disinterested enthusiasm, absorption in a compelling task or cause, a sense of elation, of being caught up in something that transcends [metaphorically] all petty, private or material concerns … of *holding true* to a principle, person or ideal'.[4] And of having an ethical attitude towards the event too, ethics being understood here as that which helps to literally en-*courage* the subject to 'keep going'; to not 'give up on your desire', to have a selfless, disinterested devotion to a cause. Such *events* are therefore the immediate catalysts that bring to fruition previously developing tendencies and concretise previous intimations of a position which, once gained, is then held fast. As Badiou puts it:

> I shall call 'truth' [position] the real process of a fidelity to an event: that which this fidelity *produces* in the situation. For example the politics of the French Maoists between 1966 and 1976 which tried to think and practise two entangled events: the Cultural Revolution in China and May '68 in France. Or so-called 'contemporary' music ... which is fidelity to the great Viennese composers of the early twentieth century. Or the algebraic geometry of the 1950s and 1960s and so forth. Essentially a truth [position] is the material course traced, within the situation, by the eventual *supplementation* ... from the decision to relate henceforth to the situation *from the perspective of its eventual supplement* ... It is thus an *immanent break.* 'Immanent' because a truth proceeds *in* the situation, and nowhere else – there is no heaven [foundation] of truths. 'Break' because what enables the truth-process [reflexive positioning] – the event – means nothing according to the prevailing language and established knowledge ...[5]

This innovation, this truth, this position which *'punches a "hole" in established knowledges'*, produces a position that is, as it were, *induced* by the *event* (aprés Rorty, the notion of 'giving birth to oneself'), after which one has to rework one's previously *ordinary* ways of being into *newness*:

> It is clear that under the effect of a loving encounter [event] if I want to be *really* faithful to it, I must completely rework my ordinary way of 'living' my situation. If I want to be faithful to the event of the 'Cultural Revolution', then I must at least practise politics ... in an entirely different manner from that proposed by the socialist and trade unionists' traditions. Again, Berg and Webern, faithful to the musical event known by the name of 'Schoenberg', cannot continue with *fin de siècle* neo-Romanticism as if nothing had happened. And after Einstein's texts of 1905 if I am faithful to their radical novelty I cannot continue to practise physics within its classical framework, and so on. An eventual

fidelity is a real break (both thought and practised) in the specific order within which the event takes place (be it political, loving, artistic or scientific).[6]

And so, if I want to be faithful to the 'posts' – to post-structuralism, post-colonialism, post-feminism, post-modernism – then *I cannot* in good faith remain a structuralist, a colonialist, a feminist, a modernist ... I have to break with these; commit an act of infidelity. I have to be loyal to the new. Not loyal, of course, in the sense of refusing to ever move again – for in Badiou the effort to impose a total or unqualified position or truth is considered 'evil'. But loyal to the new position that completes the break with the old, loyal to its possibilities, and loyal to the idea of endlessly reworking them save, with Derrida, that one never gives up on that one great, 'underpinning', fictional narrative ... that great *fable* of emancipation.

Continue, now, to think further along these lines. And this time think of the possibilities for the interminable refiguring opened up by the fabular nature of histories. In his *The Illusion of the End*[7] (which, if it 'punches a hole in reality'; which, if it is perceived as a text that is meaningless or void from the perspective of those who dominate the situation can have the status of an 'event') Jean Baudrillard argues that the end of the illusion of the end (i.e., the end of the illusion that 'the before now' before historicisation had an end *in* it), of the end of what was only ever a simulation of a linear past as history, offers us at least the possibility of imagining what he calls a 'poetic reversibility of events' precisely because of the as yet unexplored possibilities contained in the particular language games we inhabit, and yet which we can still think newness through as we seek to go beyond them; break them and break with them. For today we clearly recognise that, as we have seen, it is only the grammar of our language that allowed us to create in the first place grammatical (i.e, coherent) historicisations of 'the before now'; it did not allow us to discover them. Today we recognise, again to recall, that the world always *obeys* our syntax and that 'its' semantics are always only ours. And so think now of a different grammar, a different syntax, which may give rise to different ways of ordering things; to new syntactical/semantic figures. And let me follow Baudrillard for a little while as he develops what he calls a new poetics of 'history', commenting on it in passing.

For Baudrillard, then, 'the before now' has never unfolded in (say) a linear fashion as part of some kind of inherent structure or in line with some sort of evolutionary or narrative process: the 'before now' knows nothing of our geometries. Linearity is thus (like all other figures that bear the insignia of *realism*) an illusion derived from another illusion; namely, that language also unfolds in a linear fashion. For it does not. Linguistically, everything moves in loops, tropes, inversions of meaning. Discursively, linguistically, things do not relate to each other logically except in artificial (say digital) languages which are, for that very reason, 'precisely not languages'.

In which case, says Baudrillard, might we not freely transpose new language games onto the phenomenon of 'the before now'; I mean, there is obviously no-thing to stop us. And not just transpose the major figures of metaphor (metonymy, synecdoche, irony) but also those 'puerile, formalistic games ... which are the delight of the vulgar imagination: *anagrams, acrostics, spoonerisms, rhyme, strophe* and *catastrophe*'.[8] In which case, argues Baudrillard, could we not imagine and construct, for example, an *anagrammatic* history 'where meaning is dismembered and scattered to the wind, like the name of God in the anagram', or a *rhyming* history which can be read in either direction. Could we not think of 'the before now' as organised in the structure of an *acrostic* (where the initial and final letters of lines make different words and sense irrespective and underivable from the words (content) in between). Or through the form of *strophe* whereby a group of lines are detached from the rest of a poem to form a sense of sense which is underived from the immediate context or the full poem (think microhistories here) ... and so on and so forth. Is it even possible, queries Baudrillard, that such forms, which draw attention to the ways material actuality is organised through language, draws our gaze to that language and to the ways in which it *materialises* into meaning otherwise meaninglessness; indeed, is it possible that 'knowing all about' such organising, artificial and arbitrary syntactical grids might allow us to see the world anew and even to confront 'the radical illusion of the world' stripped of our old organising metaphors and allegories and thus ready to be re-allegorised into fresh meanings... a process we know we can *begin again*, over and over? Well, if this were possible then such would be, as Baudrillard puts it, 'the enchanted alternative to the linearity of history', the poetic alternative of refiguring, as reflexively as possible, that which has already been figured into those 'reality effects' we have forgotten are mere effects and think of as reality.

And yet we must be careful that in our possible enthusiasm for the new we never forget that these are merely the effects of the new; that there is no 'reality' here save by virtue of them. Alongside Baudrillard, Elizabeth Ermarth has cautioned against us becoming immersed, yet again, in 'the depths of the past'. In various articles in which Ermarth considers the possibility of still making history when its modernist apparatus of consensual values of neutrality/objectivity have been undercut, and when its epistemological and methodological fetishisms have been dismantled not just philosophically but 'by the postmodern world', she draws upon the notion of *anthematic* recognition in Vladimir Nabokov's works and on the term *anthemion* which, for Nabokov, refers to those inter-laced, flower-like designs where items and patterns arrive and depart seemingly from all over the place, occurring and reoccurring without exact repetition, and yet which produce a kind of rhythmic patterning where, for Nabokov as for Ermarth, there lie, metaphorically 'beneath' such rhythms, 'tender intervals within which opportunities lie and the sum of which constitutes memory and experience: postmodern experience'. From this perspective the recovery of 'the before now' as striven for in modernist histories – 'the attempt to keep the whole world in mind' as Ermarth puts it – is increasingly difficult, not least in a multi-cultural and multi-national world bereft of both foundational grand and petite narratives, such that the *anthematic* alternative seems not just an attractive but an almost unavoidable alternative. For in this construal, says Ermarth,

> The unprecedented and unrepeatable event is the potential beginning of anthematic development, each a specification of a systematic potential, each with its own pattern and possible future. The sum of such anthematic development over time constitutes the continuum of an individual life. Anthematic emphasis falls precisely on the present moment, *not* as a transfer site between past and future, but as the growing point of an unpredictable anthemion of a life. Each sequence has its own possible *grammars* and specifications, its own past and trajectory.[9]

Drawing on the first chapter of Nabokov's *Transparent Things*, and in doing so adding to the concept of *anthemion* the concept of *refraction*, Ermarth tells how the narrator warns the *novices* of the book – *novice historians in this case* – to avoid sinking into the depths of the historicised past, modernist style, and to remain very precisely on the surface of things. Thus Nabokov writes:

> When we concentrate on a material object, whatever its situation, the very act of attention may lead to our involuntary sinking into the history of that object. [But history] novices must learn to skim over matter if they want to stay at the exact level of the moment. Transparent things, through which the past shines!
>
> [Of course] man-made objects, or natural ones, inert in themselves but much used by careless life … are particularly difficult to keep in surface focus: novices [easily] fall through the surface [of the now] humming happily to themselves, and are soon revelling with child-like abandon in the [history] of *this* stone, the [history] of *that* heath. I shall explain. A thin veneer of immediate reality is spread over natural and artificial matter, and whoever wishes to remain in the now, with the now, should not break its tension film. Otherwise the inexperienced [history novice] … will find himself no longer walking on water but descending upright among staring fish.[10]

To which Ermarth glosses Nabokov thus:

> The powers required to pursue history destroy the past by sinking into it; allowing the past to *refract* through 'transparent things' requires a discipline as miraculous as that of walking on water but nevertheless possible for the [historian] novice … who learns by staying at the exact level of the moment, letting the past shine through. 'Things' no longer function as they did in the objectifying grammars of modernity; 'things' are not 'objects' but instead, the occasions, the carriers, the sites where the act of attention can be performed, where memory [experience] inflects and reinflects again; an imaginative awareness engaged in the process of creating the unique and unrepeatable poetry of a life.[11]

And let me now gloss Ermarth and work her comment that our attitude toward historicisation should be *refractive*. Thus, let us imagine the past as a medium of different density which we can only ever enter obliquely in the present: what we see under and through the 'surface' is never quite in the right place; there is always a *dis-location* (as when we put a stick in a glass of water). And so let us see historicisations of the past as precisely these kinds of *fractures*, as breaks between the now and the then which can never be – nor should we ever bother about them ever being – healed up into a full, unbroken meaning. And let our *attitude* towards historical orthodoxy be *refractory*; that is, *cantankerous, contentious, difficult, disobedient, disputatious, disrespectful, headstrong, intractable, obstinate, unruly*; let us embody our *Thesaurus*. Let us stay on the surface and skim. Let us trick with our tropes, plot and emplot, figure and refigure in poetic arrangements that resist codification and the death-knell of orthodoxy … let us be – who knows …?

For those who can think in this way, the postmodern way of Baudrillard and Ermarth, it now becomes inconceivable to think of a historical consciousness that remains sunk in the depths of the realist/ epistemological mind-set of modernist historians – however *reflective*. Postmodernism, to this way of thinking, is not some sort of fashion, nor some kind of critical discourse that can be ignored or recuperated back into modernity in the guise of 'pluralistic interpretations' once its excesses are shed: for postmodernism *is* its excesses; *postmodernism is everything modernity cannot ever be*. Postmodernism, as understood positively here, is the getting of an attitude, a militant, radical disposition, that undercuts not just the content but the grammatical forms of modernist histories without a hint of nostalgia and offers in their place, in its new grammars and acts of attention, new ways of rendering up 'the before now' as yet unconceived of. *Modernist histories and historians fade away and disappear here.* So that to those modernists who think that history is still an epistemology rather than a reflexive, aestheticising, figuring, grammatically promiscuous, *refractive* discursive experiment without foundations – and that to it postmodernism makes no difference – all I can say finally is: think about it. And then relax. And then go with it. I mean, why not? You have nothing to lose but your pasts.

CODA

Coda. A postcript. A script past/post the script you have just read; an etcetera. An etcetera of a certain kind. Because a writer is never sure if, having 'read' the script, the reader has 'got it'. 'Got it' not in the sense of closing it and everything else down but 'got it' enough to know where the writer stands and so where to move on from. And so I want to make three points which try to pull together some of the implications, for me at least, of standing here.

The first is to underline the fact that critics of postmodern histories generally pose to its proposers the kinds of questions which – and this is the point – can now be very clearly seen as redundant. These are questions which, no matter how put, all boil down to concerns about objectivity, disinterest, truth and relativism which, again boiled down, effectively take the following familiar form: if postmodern histories are aesthetic, figurative discourses without foundations, then what happens to the pursuit of truth at the end of enquiry? And my reply is to say that if the notion of the aesthetic is really understood then nobody could possibly ask this epistemological-type question any more. There is no point. And this for the inescapable reason that it is no good expecting an aesthetic to be able to answer epistemological questions. For the difference between these two phenomena is precisely an ontological one; that is, aesthetics and epistemologies are different not in degree but in kind. And this explains why the break between modernist and postmodernist histories is not an 'epistemological break' (which seems to allow for the possibility that one day they might be 'joined up' and healed over) but a permanent, because incommensurable, difference.

Second, it therefore follows that it is no good thinking that post-modernist insights – insights into language, representation, narratology, etc., – can be somehow grafted onto modernist histories which might allow them to overcome postmodern 'critiques' and thus survive intact. For this is not possible; the break between modernity and postmodernity is as epochal, I think, as that between the medieval and the modern, and it is as inconceivable to think that modernists will be able to survive in postmodernity any more than medievalists might be expected to survive in modernity; these are just different worlds.

Moreover, it is also a profound mistake for academic historians to think that postmodernists want their kind of epistemological history to continue and that they may even want to help them to do so. It is, of course, understandable that such historians, mistaking their genre of history for the 'Real Thing', can see no alternative to their practices, but postmodernists can and do, and such sightings signal the end of one type of history and the beginning of others – as yet embryonic. Postmodernity offers new births.

Third and finally, from a postmodern perspective this unavoidable break is a break which, though understandable 'historically' is, logically, a break which should never have been made in the first place. For if postmodernist claims regarding what is arguably the best way of characterising histories – as aesthetic, figurative discourses – are correct, then it is not that postmodern histories alone are examples of an aestheticisation of the past which then stand over against modernist ones which just happen not to be aesthetic. For if history as such seems always to have been and always will be an aesthetic, then there have never been histories of any other type. All histories always have been and always will be aesthetic, figurative discourses; all histories are thus of the aesthetic type postmodernists raise to consciousness. Which is another way of saying that postmodernism is 'the only game in town'. So that in coming to the end of epistemological histories we have as it were come home to ourselves. And so let us accept this homecoming; this happiest of thoughts which can at this point be thrown into the wake: epistemological histories just ought never to have existed; histories ought never to have been modern.

Notes

Introduction

1 Postmodernism has many different definitions. In this text I have decided to think of it as 'the era of the aporia'. By aporia I mean that this is an era when all the decisions we take – political, ethical, moral, interpretive, representational, etc., are ultimately undecidable (aporetic). That our chosen ways of seeing things lack foundations and that, as far as a discourse like history is concerned, it is essentially to be thought of as an aesthetic – a shaping, figuring discourse – and not as an objective, true, or foundational epistemology. And this definition fits in with the argument of this text.

2 I have discussed most of these theorists in my earlier *On 'What is History?'* (London, Routledge, 1995).

3 Richard Evans, *In Defence of History* (London: Granta, 2nd edition 2001); Arthur Marwick, *The New Nature of History* (London, Palgrave, 2001).

4 Ernesto Laclau, 'The uses of equality' in *Diacritics* (Spring, 1997), pp. 3–17. See for an extended discussion of radical democracy, J. Butler, E. Laclau and S. Žižek, *Contingency, Hegemony, Universality* (London, Verso, 2000).

5 I have discussed the failure of the modernist experiment in *On 'What is History?'*, op cit. *passim*.

6 *Rethinking History*, with a new preface and an interview by Alun Munslow, will be published in the Routledge Classics series in early 2003.

I Opening time(s)

1 Quoted in M. Poster, *Cultural History and Postmodernity* (Berkeley, University of California Press, 1996), p. 110.

2 Quoted in E. Ermarth, *Sequel to History* (Princeton, Princeton University Press, 1992), p. 148.

3 Ibid., p. 184.

4 Derrida has spelt out the idea of the 'undecidability of the decision' in many places, but most accessibly in two short essays and an interview. Thus, see his 'Remarks on Deconstruction and Pragmatism' in C. Mouffe (ed.) *Pragmatism and Deconstruction* (London, Routledge, 1996), pp. 77–88; 'Deconstructions: The Im-possible' in S. Lotringer and S. Cohen (eds), *French Theory in America* (London, Routledge, 2001), pp. 13–32; 'The Deconstruction of Actuality' in *Radical Philosophy*, 68 (1994). See also Laclau's comments on Derrida's undecidability in his 'Deconstruction, Pragmatism, Hegemony' in Mouffe, pp. 47–68.

5 See Derrida's interview with R. Kearney 'Deconstruction and the Other', *States of Mind* (Manchester, Manchester University Press, 1995), pp. 156–76, p. 170; here Derrida writes: 'I try where I can to act politically while recognising that such action remains incommensurate with my intellectual project of deconstruction'.

6 J. Derrida, 'Spectres of Marx' in *New Left Review*, 205 (1994), p. 53.

7 J. F. Lyotard, *The Postmodern Condition* (Manchester, Manchester University Press, 1984), Appendix.

8 S. Cohen, *Historical Culture* (Berkeley, University of California Press, 1986), p. 2.

9 J. Baudrillard, *The Perfect Crime* (London, Verso, 1996), *passim*. See also my chapter on 'Baudrillard and History' in *Why History?*, ibid., pp. 56–70.

10 R. Beardsworth, *Derrida and the Political* (London, Routledge, 1996), p. xiii.

11 Some of my argument here is taken from my 'A Postmodern Reply to Perez Zagorin' in *History and Theory*, 39, 2 (2000), pp. 181–200. For introductions to Derrida in general, the very best is probably G. Bennington's *Interrupting Derrida* (London, Routledge, 2000). Bennington's *Jacques Derrida* (written with Derrida) (Chicago, University of Chicago Press, 2nd edition, 1999) is another excellent text, containing a near one-hundred-page bibliography of works on and by Derrida. See also S. Critchley's *The Ethics of Deconstruction* (Edinburgh, Edinburgh University Press, 2nd edition, 1999) and his *Ethics, Politics, Subjectivity* (London, Verso, 1999).

12 J. Derrida in Mouffe, op. cit., pp. 83–4.

13 One of the clearest introductions to Derrida and language is Critchley's *The Ethics of Deconstruction*, op. cit; see especially chapters one and two.

14 Derrida quoted in Bennington, ibid., p. 37.

15 ibid., p. 37.

16 J. Derrida in R. Kearney, op. cit., p. 25.

2 Last order(s)

1 H. White, *Tropics of Discourse* (Baltimore, Johns Hopkins University Press, 1978), p. 47.

2 E. Laclau (J. Butler) 'The Uses of Equality', *Diacritics*, Spring (1997), pp. 3–20, p. 18.

3 M. Roth, *The Ironist's Cage* (New York, Columbia University Press, 1995).

4 E. Domanska, *Encounters: Philosophy of History After Postmodernism* (Charlottesville, University Press of Virginia, 1998), p. 17. Domanska's book – a series of interviews with leading historians/history theorists (White, Kellner, Ankersmit, Iggers, Topolski, Rusen, Danto, Gossman, Burke and Bann) – offers some invaluable insights into the theorists and motivations of key contributors to 'postmodernism and history'.

5 K. Jenkins, 'A Conversation with Hayden White', *Literature and History*, 3rd series, 7, 1 (1998), pp. 71–2.

6 A. Danto, *Analytical Philosophy of History* (Cambridge, Cambridge University Press, 1965), pp. 143–81. Danto also puts this argument forward in a slightly different way in 'Narrative Sentences', *History and Theory*, 11 (1962), pp. 146–79. See also his, 'The Decline and Fall of The Analytical Philosophy of History' in F. R. Ankersmit and H. Kellner (eds) *A New Philosophy of History* (London, Reaktion Press, 1995), pp. 70–88; the whole volume is an excellent introduction to history beyond 'the linguistic turn'.

7 F. R. Ankersmit, *History and Tropology* (Berkeley, University of California Press, 1994), p. 187 *passim*.

8 F. R. Ankersmit, op. cit., p. 190. For White's definition of history as a narrative discourse as much imagined as found, see his essay 'The Historical Text as Literary Artefact' in *Tropics of Discourse*, op. cit., pp. 81–100, p. 82 and p. 2 of his *Metahistory* (Baltimore, Johns Hopkins University Press, 1973).

9 H. White, 'Historical Emplotment and the Problem of Truth in Historical Representation' in *Figural Realism* (Baltimore, Johns Hopkins University Press, 1999), pp. 27–42, p. 27.

10 R. Barthes, 'The Discourse of History' in K. Jenkins, *The Postmodern History Reader* (London, Routledge, 1997), pp. 120–3.

11 C. Lorenz, 'Historical Knowledge and Historical Reality' in *History and Theory*, 33, 3 (1994), pp. 297–334, pp. 313–14.

12 R. Berkhofer, 'The Challenge of Poetics to (Normal) Historical Practice' in K. Jenkins, *The Postmodern History Reader*, op. cit., pp. 139–57, pp. 146–7.

13 H. White, 'An Old Question Raised Again: Is Historiography Art or Science?' in *Rethinking History Journal*, 4, 3 (2000), pp. 391–406, p. 392.

14 F. R. Ankersmit, *Historical Representation* (forthcoming 2002); 'Reply to

Professor Zagorin', *History and Theory*, 29, 3 (1990).
15 F. R. Ankersmit, 'Reply to Professor Zagorin', ibid., p. 277.
16 Ibid., p. 278.
17 Ankersmit, *Historical Representation*.
18 Ibid.
19 Ibid.
20 H. White, *Metahistory*, op. cit., p. 433.

3 Beginning again: on disobedient dispositions

1 E. Said, *Representations of the Intellectual* (London, Vintage, 1994), p. 9.
2 Ibid., p. 46.
3 P. Hallward, 'Introduction to A. Badiou', *Ethics: An Essay on the Understanding of Evil* (London, Verso, 2001), p. viii.
4 Ibid., p. x.
5 Ibid., p. 42.
6 Ibid., p. 42.
7 J. Baudrillard, *The Illusion of the End* (Cambridge, Polity Press, 1994). See especially Baudrillard's last two (very) short chapters in which he outlines his new 'poetics of history'.
8 Ibid., pp. 120–2.
9 E. D. Ermarth, 'Beyond "The Subject": Individuality in the Discursive Condition', *New Literary History*, 31, 3 (2000), pp. 405–20. Ermarth has developed her ideas – discussed at length in her *Sequel to History: Postmodernism and the Crisis of Representational Time* (Princeton, Princeton University Press, 1992) – in various places. See her 'Phrase Time: Chaos Theory and Postmodern Reports on Knowledge', *Time and Society*, 4 (1995), pp. 95–100; 'Time and Neutrality: Media of Modernity in a Postmodern World', *Cultural Values*, 1 (1998), pp. 355–67. Ermarth has written a brief but incisive intellectual/biographical essay (Beyond History) for *Rethinking History Journal*, 5, 2 (2001), pp. 195–215. Ermarth is, I think, one of the very few writers who take the end of modernity's histories for granted and who is interested, above all, in 'the possibilities for writing histories once the consensus apparatus supporting modernity has been dismantled? This question is currently engaging me . . .' (*Beyond History*, p. 212).
10 V. Nabokov, *Transparent Things* (London, Weidenfeld and Nicolson, 1973), pp. 1–2.
11 Ermarth, 'Beyond "the Subject"', op. cit., p. 417.

Index